D0897684

THE ALPHABET CONNECTION

THE ALPHABET CONNECTION

A Parent's and Teacher's Guide to Beginning Reading and Writing

Pam Palewicz-Rousseau
and
Lynda Madaras

SCHOCKEN BOOKS • NEW YORK

First published by SCHOCKEN BOOKS 1979

Library of Congress Cataloging in Publication Data

Palewicz-Rousseau, Pam.

The alphabet connection.

Bibliography: p.
Includes index
1. Reading—Handbooks, manuals, etc. 2. Books and reading for children—Handbooks, manuals, etc. I. Madaras, Lynda, joint author. II. Title.
LB1050.M343 372.4 79-12493

Credits:

Illustrations: Ann Mulkey and the students of Sequoyah School, Pasadena, California

Photographs: Maury Cohen

The Basic Vocabulary List in the Appendix is abridged from *Improving Reading Instruction* by Donald Durrell, copyright©1956, 1940 by Harcourt Brace Jovanovich, Inc. Reprinted by permission of the publisher.

The photograph on page 25 is reprinted from *Child's Play* by Lynda Madaras, copyright©1977 by Peace Press of Culver City, California. Reprinted by permission of the publisher.

DEDICATION

My half of this dedication goes to Miss Maiser (we never heard of "Ms." in those days), who was my seventh-grade teacher. One day, out of the clear, blue sky, she charged through the door of the classroom in a curious, side-stepping motion, leaning at an impossible and precarious angle, and screamed, "The axis of the earth is tilted at a 23½-degree angle." When she got to her desk, she straightened up and announced to her stunned students, "That's one fact you'll never forget." She was right. Another day, when I was acting rowdy in the back row, she jumped up, pointed her finger at me, and bellowed, "When I was your age, I was just like you and my teacher pronounced a curse upon me which I, in turn, now inflict on you: May you grow up to become a teacher and have a student just like you in your class." So, this is for you, Ms. Maiser, wherever you are.

—L.M.

I dedicate my half of this book to myself, who deserves it, and to those who have helped me along. And also to those who've stood in my way, 'cause after all, it's what we've done that makes us who we are.

—P.P.R.

ACKNOWLEDGMENTS

We have a whole herd of human beings to thank:

First, the unsung, but oh-so-essential heroes, our typists, Alma Collins and Ann Worth. Next, our underpaid, starving artists, Ann Mulkey, the illustrator, and Maury Cohen, the photographer. Then, the staff of the Altadena Public Library, for letting us run a tab; George Madaras, for thinking up the title; Jean Madsen, for everything; Richard Johnson, for valor in the last, desperate proofreading; Wally Palewicz, for making one of us possible; Carol Vogel, for not making it in the last dedication; Seymour Barofsky, for giving us a deadline so we aren't still writing and rewriting this book; Harold Moskovitz, our agent, for keeping us in cherry bon-bons.

And, last but not least, the staff and students of Sequoyah School in Pasadena, California:

The Tall People: Hannah MacLaren, Lou Ann Sobieski, Carolyn Frayer, Joe Titizian, Barbra Burquest, Janet Jacobson, Michael Madsen, and Toby Manzanares.

The Short People: Area, Rebecca, Morgan, Dylan, Danya, Maya, Mo, Jennifer, Rebecca, Shoshi, William, Erin, Brianna, Lisa, Jeremy, Lisa, Bryan, Markie, Abigail, Amanda, Eric, Adam, Sebastian, Eden, Desiree, Laurie, Ann, Christian, Kerry, Thomas, Duck the Rat, Maisha, Kenny, Craig, Jerry, Edward, Lorin, Peter, Pricilla, Peter, Aldo, Piero, Tracie, Joshua, Gabriella, Mark, Paul, Laurel, Todd, John, David, Carl, Dennis, Matthew, Christy, Lauren, Holly, Ratty, Bun Buns, Mark, Amy, Duane, Laurice, David, Michal, Michael, Chandra, Yogin, Colin, Michelle, Michael, Dane Christopher, Courtenay, Abie, Diego, Lisa, Jenny, Peter, Susy, Dennis, Shalom, David, Nicole, Robby, Jordan, Grady, Sarah, Flora, and Lil Joe. Thanks to all of you.

CONTENTS

I LOVE MY SCHOOL

1

BEYOND DICK AND JANE

Until fairly recently, most children learned to read with Dick and Jane, or with similar characters whose names and identities were only slightly different. Whatever the particular names or characters, these reading primers had at least one thing in common: They were unbearably boring. It's hard to imagine how a child could have worked up sufficient interest to learn to read with such materials. "Run, Dick, run" and "Look, Jane, see Dick run" are not exactly high adventure. The language is formal and stilted, a style of speech that no child hears or uses.

Of course, most schools have replaced the old Dick and Jane–type readers. Unfortunately, most of the replacements aren't much better. Dick may have darker skin; Jane may get a chance to run, too. Such books may have gotten away from the my-mother-the-mop syndrome somewhat; Mother isn't *always* in the kitchen cooking and cleaning. For the most part, though, it's the same stilted language and ho-hum adventures.

When we landed our first teaching jobs, we were faced with the rather dreary task of having to choose reading primers for our classrooms. Even the best of what was available seemed woefully inadequate. Oh, there were some that were suitably nonsexist or nonracist, but the stories seemed to lack the drama and energy that fill the lives of young children. These reading books conjured up memories of our own deadly dull school days spent staring out the classroom window or counting the seemingly endless minutes on the wall clock. The thought of reliving, or worse yet, re-creating that boredom, now that we were teachers ourselves, was intolerable.

The Key Word and Story Approach to Reading

In our student teaching days, we had worked with high school dropouts who had never learned to read. These street-wise kids were not about to be seen poring over a book about Dick and Jane, so we had them tape-record their own stories, which we typed up and used as reading texts. We had gotten such wonderful results with this approach that we felt sure something along the same lines would work with younger children.

We were lucky enough to come across a book entitled *Teacher* by Sylvia Ashton-Warner (Simon & Schuster, 1963). In this book, the author describes her work in New Zealand with a group of Maori youngsters. Coming into the unfamiliar white culture's school and language was a problem for these children. Failure in school was common. Ms. Ashton-Warner felt the available reading materials were not at all appropriate; the cultural gap was far too wide. So, in an effort to provide reading materials that reflected the Maori culture, she developed an approach to reading that involved having the children choose a vocabulary word and dictate (and later write) a story about that word.

Thus, we began our reading program with a simple set of white index cards on which we printed the words that our children chose. The words they chose were nothing like "Run, Spot, run. See the ball"—emotionally sterile words that could hardly inspire a love of language. Instead, when we reached into the children's minds, out came vivid, exciting words like *kiss, love, monster, fight*—words that were intense and meaningful. These vocabularies were alive. They came from within and were tied to the dynamics of the child's life.

"Children," Ms. Ashton-Warner tells us, "have two visions, the inner and the outer. Of the two, the inner vision is much brighter." Adult-written books and adult-chosen vocabularies, no matter how wonderfully constructed, can never have the same energy as the words that come from the child's inner world. Such words, which we now refer to as Key Words, don't have to be drilled into children's memories. They are learned instantly because they are already charged with meaning for the child.

Instead of relying on standardized reading books, we let the kids dictate, and later write, their own stories. Human beings, big or little, are endowed with an absorbing self-interest. What could be more interesting to children than stories written by them, about themselves?

The stories they write themselves are nothing like the stories in the usual primary reading books. In child-authored stories, the world is not so fine or simple as in the Dick and Jane–type readers, where the sun always shines and no one ever cries or falls down and gets hurt or bleeds or hears monsters under the bed at night or worries about Mommy and Daddy getting a divorce or laughs long and hard or experiences joy and delight. In child-authored books, it storms and blows; ghosts, monsters, and devils abound; mommies and daddies hug and kiss and fight; grandparents and pet kittens die; hummingbirds alight on window sills in the early morning; sibling rivalries simmer. Life, real life, with all its wild disorders, all its ups and downs, all its hard times and good times, pours forth from the stories children write. As Sylvia Ashton-Warner points out, the distance between the real life of a child and life of the characters in primary reading books is frightening. So much feeling is ignored and repressed. Perhaps that's why such books are so unbearably boring.

Our experience has shown us that kids who learn to read with words and stories of their own choosing are doing a lot more than merely learning how to decode the written symbols that represent speech. They are learning how to bring the visions of their inner world fearlessly and openly to the outer world. They are learning to express themselves in written language, to communicate their thoughts and feelings, to share their dreams and ideas with others. They learn that language is powerful and meaningful, not an empty bag full of polite conventions and meaningless chatter.

Take, for instance, this poem dictated by a seven-year old child in our class whose parents had been recently divorced:

Among the trees
Everyone has birth
And everyone dies
The trees, though, live on
And I do not wish for death.

There is a tree
That has been there
Almost always
Since I was born.

I used to climb
With my mother
Sitting in her lap
Looking at the stars
Up above us
And looking at the city
Down below.
My father would come, too.
Now that they have separated
My mother and I go.

I'll remember that tree
All my life.
I believe
There's an angel
Deep inside the bark.
Among all that trash
And beer cans
And dirt
Lies a beautiful land.
That, I'll never forget.

This child did not learn to read with Dick and Jane readers. Her first experience with words were personal and powerful. They were words that came from within, words that had power for her. Perhaps her natural talent would have survived the boredom and sterility of traditional teaching methods. Perhaps the usual lessons in composition would not have reduced her to pleasant, dull, dutifully composed themes and thoughts. Still, we can't help thinking that her introduction to reading and writing had something to do with helping what is, in our opinion, a very powerful talent, grow.

Phonics vs. the Whole-Word Method

The Key Word approach to teaching reading, which we have adapted and devised and revised over the years and which is described in chapters 4 and 6 of this book, forms the basis of our approach to teaching. But we have found that, for most children, it is not enough in and of itself. The Key Word approach is a whole-word approach to teaching reading, and we have found that most children need work with phonics as well.

Perhaps we should explain this a bit more fully. Basically,

there are two ways to teach beginning reading: the whole-word method and the phonic method. The whole-word method, or the "look and say" method as it is sometimes called, is pretty much what the name implies—teaching kids to recognize, by sight, an entire word. The phonic method involves teaching the various sounds that letters make and how to blend them together to form words.

Perhaps you remember word flash cards that had a word like *apple* printed in bold type with a picture of a bright red apple underneath. These kinds of materials are used in the whole-word method of teaching reading. It is a method that has fallen in and out of favor throughout the history of educaton. At the moment, it's pretty much on the outs.

More likely, you remember learning to "sound out" words. In short, that's the phonic method. Usually phonics instruction begins with learning to associate a single sound with each letter of the alphabet. Later, the sounds made by combinations of letters and all the different sounds that a single letter can make are introduced along with the rules governing what letter makes what sound when (and all the exceptions to those rules). Then, somewhere along the line (and it varies from program to reading program) the student is taught to blend these sounds together to form words.

The debate as to which is the best method has been the subject of endless pieces of educational research, national symposia, and teachers' conferences. And, of course, all the experts disagree. Proponents of the whole-word method argue that English is not a phonetic language so there are as many exceptions to the rule as there are rules. For example, consider the rules governing the sounds made by the letters *th* in combination:

> The letters *th* together form a digraph (a combination of letters that makes a single sound). This digraph can be voiced, as in baths, or voiceless, as in bath. The final *th* is usually voiceless except smooth, with, and in *the* endings as, for example, bathe. Some verbs drop the final *e* but still follow the rule—moth, bequeath, and smooth. Some nouns with a voiceless singular (mouth) have a voiced plural.

Generally when the final *ths* is preceded by a short vowel sound (deaths) or by a consonant (months), it is unvoiced. The words cloths, truths, youths, and wreaths may have either. Initial *th* in such words as the, them, there, this, and thither is voiced. *Th* in Thomas, Esther, and Thompson is simply a *t*.

Obviously phonics can get pretty ridiculous. Still, as phonics teachers will argue, a child needs some kind of guidelines or tools for attacking new words as he comes across them (and they always call it "word-attack skills," as if words were enemies to be assaulted). The debate between proponents of these two approaches has, at times, gotten rather vehement. At the moment, though, the experts seem to be at pretty much of a draw and it is now considered acceptable to use a combination of both methods, which makes us feel pretty good, since that's what we've always done.

In addition to the Key Word Cards and Stories, we've developed a number of different games, exercises, and activities based on both phonic and whole-word methods. This game approach to learning has proven quite effective for us. Kids learn best when they are having fun. Many kids will happily play Go Fish for hours on end. But how many will cheerfully study and memorize new words for hours? Obviously, not too many. So we make a deck of Go Fish cards with words instead of suits and numbers. That way, the hours spent playing are also hours spent learning.

Parents as Teachers

Once we had developed our own style of teaching reading, we felt more comfortable about answering the questions and pleas for advice that came from friends and parents of children in our kindergarten and preschool classes: "My child wants to learn to read—what should I do?" or "My child is having trouble learning to read—how can I help?"

Traditionally, parents and other nonprofessionals have been discouraged from teaching kids to read or from tutoring their own children if they are having problems. Supposedly, this could do great harm. Better to leave the matter in the hands of state-certified teachers, who are supposedly experts in these matters. One wonders. As John Holt, the well-known educator, has pointed out, it's a good thing we haven't decided to let the schools teach our kids to walk. It would be tragic to have as many cripples as we do nonreaders.

From our experience, most parents make wonderful teachers, especially with this Key Word and game approach. The Key Word method depends on the teacher's or other adult's establishing a certain trust with the child. If there is such trust, then the child will admit the adult to the inner world of brightest vision where the best and most easily learned of the Key Words originate. Most parents, simply because they are parents, have an easier access to this world than we teachers, who are, at least at first, strangers. Because phonics is taught through a simple game approach, one need not be an expert to be a good teacher, just a good player.

Of course, there are always the horror stories about parents who push too hard, who are bound and determined that their little Johnny or Susie is going to be a whiz kid. There are, it's true, parents who want to impress their friends and relatives with their offspring's brilliance. There are the parents who've had all their panic buttons pushed by reading advertisements for educational toys and preschool training programs that warn them that the preschool years are the critical years and that they can make or break their kids' IQs. But these are the exceptions rather than the rule.

All in all, we feel that parents who teach their kids to read at home are much more likely to do a good job of it than teachers in the typical classroom situation. For one thing, parents can quite easily individualize instruction, and this creates a much healthier situation for learning. In most schools, there are thirty to forty kids in a class and only one teacher. Most teachers cope with the overpopulation in their classroom by dividing the kids into reading groups. They put the faster learners in one group and the slower learners in another, usually giving them names like "Robins" or "Pigeons" to disguise their true nature. Of course, it isn't too long before everybody knows that the Robins are the smarties and the Pigeons are the dummies. Needless to say, this doesn't have a very good effect on the Pigeons or, for that matter, on the Robins either.

It's a pretty heavy blow to the self-esteem of a six-year-old to find that he has been judged and found wanting. This kind of cut to a kid's self-confidence can be so discouraging that it robs him of the pleasure of mastering the skill of reading—and all because his rate of learning doesn't match that of the next kid's. The Robins—the faster learners—even though they are winning the game, can be just as damaged by this divide and conquer approach to learning. The "I'm-better-than-you-are" attitude doesn't exactly make for healthy personalities. There's also the danger of falling into the "Goody-Two-Shoes" syndrome—always being a "good little girl or boy," the teacher's pet. Too often it is the achievement of the teacher's special acclaim rather than self-achievement that motivates a Robin. Thus, the Robin may be stuck with the lifelong habit of looking to others rather than within himself for motivation and approval. Either way, Robin or Pigeon, there's no winning when the learning game is played this way.

When instruction is individualized, done on a one-to-one basis, there is no need to compete with others. Each child's success is measured against his own progress. Each child learns at his own rate; slow learners are not penalized. And, of course, individual attention is much more effective. This can be particularly important for the parent of a child who is having difficulty learning to read in school. Such children often come up as losers in group situations. In a home environment, where instruction is individualized, the child is measured only against his own previous performance; thus, he is always a success.

With the Key Word and game approach, the classroom teacher can reap the same natural advantage of individualized instruction. Most of the games and exercises described in chapter 5 can be done independently by an individual child or by groups of children and are self-correcting. Thus, the teacher can be freed for more creative and effective one-to-one instruction with the Key Words.

The Age Factor

In addition to the rather vague objection that parents are not trained teachers and therefore can't teach their children, some experts have worried that if parents teach their preschoolers to read, they will rob their children of their precious, carefree childhood. But learning to read doesn't have to be pressurized, boring lessons; it can be fun and games, an exciting creative adventure. Traditionally, in this country, we start reading instructon at the age of six. It's really fairly arbitrary. In Russia, it's seven; in Sweden, it's five. As long as the child is willing, any age is O.K.

We've worked with parents of three-year-olds who have learned to read. Many kids are ready to read long before school age. It seems a pity not to take advantage of a preschooler's interest in learning to master that grown-up, mystical, magical ability—reading.

Of course, any parent who is thinking about helping a child learn to read should ask the kid about it first. If you get a "no" answer, respect it. If all the kids on your block can already read and that bothers you, remember that's your problem, not your kid's. If your children would rather be out running in the sun or exploring the mysteries of a blade of grass, let them. Running in the sun, hanging about the sandbox, and other forms of play are actually an important part of learning to read. In chapters 2 and 3 we discuss the importance of play and the reading readiness skills that will help prepare children for reading.

Rewards and Bribes

The fact that we don't use standard reading primers and vocabulary lists makes our approach to reading quite different from that of most teachers. The fact that we encourage parents to teach their preschoolers and tutor children who are having difficulties in school also sets us apart from educators. There is one other aspect of our work that is also rather unorthodox. We don't use rewards, grades, or bribes—no gold stars, report cards, or lollipops.

Psychologists are discovering that rewards may sometimes have just the opposite of their desired effects. In some cases rewards may actually hinder kids' innate drive to learn. The famous animal psychologist H. F. Harlow did an interesting experiment with some monkeys. The monkeys were given puzzles, which they worked over and over again, persistently and flawlessly. The monkeys seemed to have an intrinsic or self-motivated interest in the puzzles. In other words, they worked the puzzles "just for the heck of it," because they liked doing it. When Harlow rewarded one group of monkeys with food for working the puzzles correctly, he found that they did not continue to work the puzzles on their own. The unrewarded monkeys, however, continued to work the puzzles over and over again.

It looks as if rewards might discourage, rather than encourage, interest. In a similar experiment, Mark R. Lepper and David Greene experimented with rewards in a nursery school.* Using a two-way mirror setup, they recorded the amount of time each child spent playing with some felt-tip markers and paper that had been set out on a play table. They divided the children who had shown an interest in the markers into three groups: "expected rewards," "unexpected rewards," and "no reward." Then they returned to the school and asked the children in each of the three groups if they would agree to draw some pictures for a visitor. The children in the "expected reward" group were promised a beribboned and starred certificate, which they would receive after they had finished drawing. The children in the "unexpected reward" group weren't promised anything, but after they had finished drawing, they were awarded a certificate. Children in the "no reward" group were simply thanked and told that they had "done a good job." One week later the experimenters returned to the school to again record how much time the children spent playing with the markers. The youngsters in

*This experiment was described in detail in "How to Turn Work into Work," *Psychology Today*, September 1974.

the "unexpected reward" and "no reward" groups showed a slight increase in the time they spent playing with the markers. The experimenters repeated this experiment and similar ones and got similar results. Each time, the children who expected rewards for doing something chose that activity less often after being rewarded.

It may be that rewards are effective in motivating people to do something they would not choose to do themselves. However, these experiments suggest that, in a case where there is an intrinsic desire, such as the children playing with the pens or the monkeys with the puzzles, offering rewards can hinder rather than heighten interest.

Children have an innate desire to learn. Bribing or rewarding them can interfere with that drive. That doesn't mean, however, that we don't give our kids lots of praise. We take pleasure in their accomplishments and communicate it to them with hugs and kisses and lots of praise.

On Beyond Dick and Jane

This Key Word and Story method of teaching reading has taken us on beyond the rather limited horizons of Dick and Jane. The powerful emotional aspect of the words and stories makes learning to read more than a mere rote process or mechanical skill. It becomes a creative and exciting adventure for both children and adults.

We hope that this book will provide information and inspirations to enable parents and friends and all would-be teachers to help children learn in a relaxed, fun-filled, even joyous manner. Perhaps if more kids learn to read in this way, there will be some big changes in our schools. Instead of factories for teaching the so-called basic skills and obedience to authority, schools could be centers for growth and creativity. Instead of just teaching reading, first-grade teachers might be teaching communication skills with cameras and videotapes.

If the changes in our technology and way of life are as incredible in the next fifty years as they have been in the last fifty, what is considered a "basic skill" may be very different. Learning to program the computer console in your living room that delivers up your breakfast, pays your bills, and teaches your lessons may be a more "basic skill" than knowing how to count change or how to read *Dick and Jane*.

Survival in tomorrow's changing world may depend more on having a healthy psyche than on any of the traditional basic skills. We believe that our approach to teaching reading helps build happier, healthier human beings. Children who are able to make a strong connection between their inner visions and the outer world will be well prepared to deal with the future, no matter what shape it takes. This book, *The Alphabet Connection*, is a way of strengthening that connection.

2

ON YOUR MARK, GET SET, GO: READING READINESS

There's a lot being written about reading readiness these days. Research experts have come up with forty-three basic skills that must be mastered (or sometimes it's twenty-six or fifty-seven or a hundred and two, depending on the expert) before a child is ready to learn to read. It's all a bit frightening. As one ad that ran in the *New York Times* promoting a preschool learning program tells us:

> Evaluating children in the forty-three basic skills is part of what the Discovery Center can do for your child. The forty-three skills embrace all the hundreds of things your child has to learn before he reaches school age. Fortunately pre-schoolers have a special genius for learning. But it disappears at the age of seven. During this short-lived period of genius, the Discovery Center helps develop his skills to Advanced Level. . . . You owe it to your child to take him to a Discovery Center today.

This ad is enough to send even the most sensible parents or early childhood teachers into a panic. After all, should little Johnny and Susie be out in the yard making mud pies, climbing trees, and lollygagging about the sandbox when they've got *hundreds of things* to learn and *forty-three basic skills* to master? Sounds as if Johnny and Susie have a lot of work to do if they're going to make it to the "Advanced Level" before their mental powers begin to fade. Shouldn't you get them indoors, sit them down, and get to work before they turn into morons at the age of seven?

No, not at all. Parents and teachers of young children, please relax. Johnny and Susie are doing just fine making mud pies and climbing trees. These basic skills that the experts are talking about are things that most children develop quite naturally and normally through their play. When Johnny is climbing a tree, he is "developing large muscle coordination." If Susie is playing with her set of toy vehicles and putting all the cars in one pile and all the trucks in another, she is "developing her classifying and sorting skills." When they're scribbling with their crayons, they're "refining their ocular-motor (eye-hand) coordination skills."

Most Johnnies and Susies don't need visits to an expensive educational center or piles of "scientifically designed," high-priced educational toys to learn these basic skills. In fact, making a program out of learning these basic skills is about as useful as giving swimming lessons to baby guppies. Of course, baby guppies have got to be in the water in order to learn to swim. Basically, that's what parents and early childhood educators can do for kids—provide an environment that has plenty of opportunities for children to exercise and develop the kinds of skills and abilities that they will need in order to learn to read.

Reading Aloud

One thing that parents and teachers can do to help get kids ready to read is quite simple—read to them! Not only does this help expand their vocabularies and extend their experiences, but it also teaches them how a book works: The pages turn from right to left from beginning to end; words are read from left to right across a page and from the top to the bottom of a page.

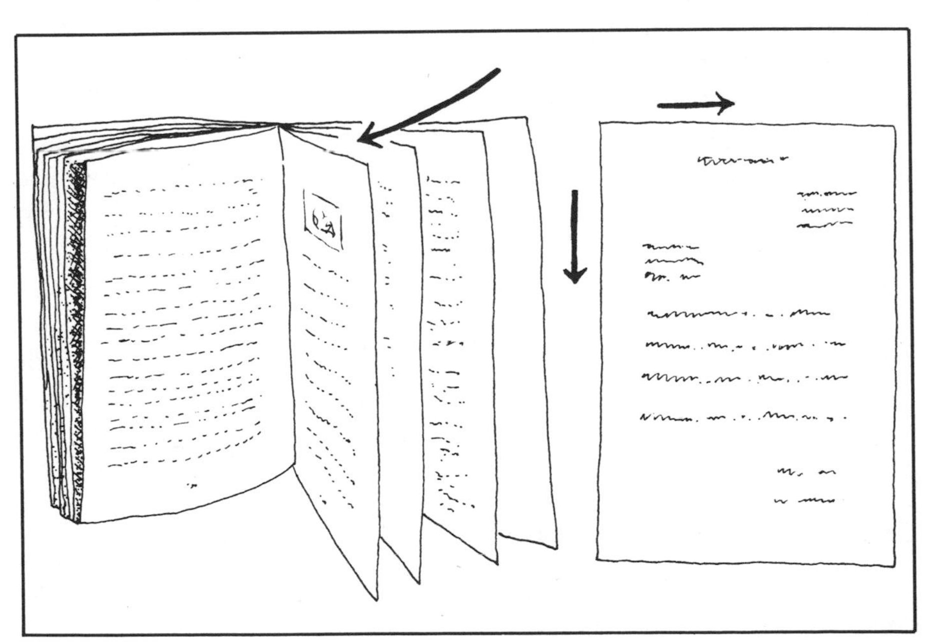

This may seem obvious to you, but it isn't so to children. Kids who have never had a book read to them have no way of knowing all of this. Moreover, it's a completely arbitrary system, so there is no reason why they should know. For instance, in Hebrew, words are read from right to left. In Chinese, the characters are read from the top to the bottom of the page. In both Hebrew and Japanese books, the pages turn from left to right. Each culture has its own way of structuring books, and children need to learn how books work in their particular cultures.

As any parent who has tried to skip a few pages in a favorite bedtime story knows, kids will memorize whole stories word for word long before they ever learn to read. We are always amused when a parent tells us, "Oh, he's not really reading that book, he's just memorized it." (*Just*?)

Even though you may be less than thrilled about reading the *Adventures of Mousie* for the thirty-fifth time, this repetition is important. As favorite stories are read over and over again and as the children memorize them, they are learning about spacing between words, sentence structure, how paragraphs and chapters are organized, not to mention logical order, sequencing of events, comprehension, and recall. They may also learn to recognize a few words by sight.

Most kids who have books read to them and are around adults who read are quite naturally interested in what books are all about. They will be delighted to have you read to them. So snuggle up and get warm and close with your child so that the associations with reading are pleasant ones. If your kid isn't interested or is busy with something else at the moment, don't force it. Wait until he is interested. Also, don't hesitate to edit or shorten a story or to simply stop reading if your child becomes fidgety or bored. After all, the point is to create interest and pleasure.

Talking about What You Read

The experience of being read to is also important because it develops a child's listening and speaking vocabularies, which are

necessary foundations for reading. Parents and teachers should try to remember that the real value of the experience lies in the development of these verbal abilities, not in the completion of the story.

Children will interrupt your reading with questions, comments, and digressions. Encourage this. The interruptions are actually more important than the story. When a kid jumps into the middle of *The Adventures of Peter Rabbit* with a story about what happened to *him* and *his* rabbit, he's getting valuable experience in verbalizing his thoughts, in thinking in logical sequences, and in adding new words to his vocabulary.

Stop from time to time before you turn the page and ask the child questions like "What do you think will happen next?"; "Which of the pictures on the page do you like best?"; "Why?"; "How do you think the character in the story feels?"; "How would you feel if it were happening to you?" This kind of analyzing is basic to comprehension and reading.

As parents, we have found it best to pick a time to read when we are feeling relaxed and leisurely, when we want to be with our children. Then we enjoy the digressions rather than see them as bothersome interruptions. We try to avoid reading only at bedtime. At bedtime we tend to be more concerned with getting through the story so we can relax ourselves. Thus, we hush the important process of questioning and commenting.

In a classroom situation it is sometimes difficult to allow such leisure. One child may be very involved in relating his comments while another may be equally involved in the story line and eager to get on to the next page. Then, too, there is the pressure of the classroom schedule, which simply won't allow for the hour and a half that it would take to accommodate everybody's unedited interruptions and digressions. Reading to a group of children is the fine art of balancing individual needs and group interest.

In our classrooms, we usually have a story time in the afternoon, at rest time. The children may play quietly by themselves with a toy, draw pictures, nap, listen to the story—whatever, as long as they don't infringe on other kids' right to listen. We don't insist that everyone pay attention to the story. It simply may not interest some of them. Often, though, the kid over in the corner who seems miles away, totally absorbed in drawing a picture, will suddenly pipe up with a question that shows he has heard every word, despite the apparent lack of attention.

Here again we aren't overly concerned with completing the story. If we've only got twenty minutes for story time and the group is caught up in a lively discussion, we encourage the discussion. We can always finish the story the next day.

Choosing Reading Materials

The bibliography in the back of this book includes some of our favorite children's books. If you are reading to a group of children, books with large and fairly simple illustrations that can be seen clearly across the room work well. There was a trend for a while to illustrate all books for young children with large, simple illustrations and bold, primary colors. Luckily, there is now a return to more intricate illustrations and subtle colors, which children are quite capable of appreciating. Parents and teachers will want to make sure that children have access to these more visually sophisticated books as well.

You needn't limit the books you select to read to your children to those with pictures on every page and simple vocabularies. Experiment with more complex books. We've read the *Wizard of Oz* stories, which have very sophisticated vocabularies and few illustrations, to three- and four-year-olds with great success. If the book you've chosen is too sophisticated, your audience will let you know by their unmistakable fidgeting that you are in over their heads.

Kids often enjoy poetry. We've read Dylan Thomas's *A Child's Christmas in Wales* to kids who loved it. The rhythm of the language alone holds their interest even if many of the words are unfamiliar. Another favorite poem is James Whitcomb Reilly's *Little Orphan Annie*, a spooky tale complete with goblins that is delightful when read by candlelight in a darkened room. Edgar Allen Poe's *The Raven* or *Anabelle Lee* are big hits too. Choose any poem that you love or a favorite passage from a book to share with your children. Often, once you explain the meaning of the unfamiliar words, the maturity of children's comments and the depth of their understanding will astound you.

Newspapers are also a good source for material to be read aloud to young children. Lead paragraphs from news stories, letters from "Dear Abby," filler items—many of these can be understood by very young children. Newspaper comic strips are great favorites, probably because of the illustrations. Of course, "Mary Worth" and "Rex Morgan" are not usually big hits, but "Peanuts" is. Unfortunately, many comic strips are extremely violent or reflect values that are not necessarily ones we want to communicate to our children. Still, such strips have a certain value, for they can open up discussion about these issues. Besides, newspapers seem very grown-up and are therefore very desirable to kids.

Add variety to the kinds of books and reading materials that you select for your children, and you'll find that reading to them becomes more pleasurable for you as well.

Talking and Listening

Another simple, but very important, thing that adults can do to help children get ready to learn reading is to talk to the kids and to listen to them. A child who comes from a home where the parents have talked to the kids, not merely baby-talked or talked down to them, is going to have a rich vocabulary. Adults should try to be specific in the language they use with children. If, for instance, the child asks "Where is my doll?" and the typical answer he gets from the adults around him is a vague, "Over there," that child will probably not develop the same language skills as the child who is answered, "It's over there in the corner, behind the blue chair." Such a child has a lot more to work with. Likewise, a child who grows up around adults who have the time and patience to listen to his often rambling discourses about what he saw or felt or thought is going to have a much greater facility with language than the child whose parents tell him to be quiet all the time.

Listening and speaking vocabularies are the foundations for reading vocabularies. From infancy on, children are developing their listening vocabularies. They can understand much of what we say, even though they cannot speak. Later, they begin to build speaking vocabularies. By listening and trying out the new words that they hear, they build their speaking vocabularies. Still later, they will develop their reading vocabularies out of their listening and speaking vocabularies.

Children cannot learn to read words they have never heard or said. We adults may be able to sound out a nonsense word like *plammer*, but we cannot really read it, for it is a nonsense word that has no meaning. In the same way, a child may develop enough phonic skill to sound out the word *cat*, but if he has never seen one, or heard or spoken the word, he will not really be able to read it, for the word has no meaning for him. A well-developed listening and speaking vocabulary, then, is essential for reading.

Creating Opportunities for Oral Language Development

Sometimes getting enough speaking experience is tricky for a young child with an older sibling. It often happens that the older brother or sister will be able to interpret the early speech of the younger one better than the parent, thus assuming the role of translator: "He says he wants a bottle, his rattle, a bath," etc. Teachers may find a similar thing happening in their classrooms when a more verbal child will do the talking for a less verbal one.

Children often form what at first glance seems to be the most unlikely alliances. Thus, the class chatterbox is best friends with the child who punctuates his silence and shyness with a thumb constantly stuck in his mouth. The shy one speaks only to and through the friend, the mouthpiece. One such couple comes to mind, two little girls who, despite our most creative and most manipulative methods, refused to end this aspect of their relationship. Finally, at wit's end, we sat them down and explained that we understood and felt good about their special friendship, but that sometimes Katie did all the talking and that didn't seem to be helping Carol, who needed to learn to talk for herself. The results of the simple discussion that followed were so astounding—Katie would actually remind Carol that she should and could say it herself—that we felt foolish about all the backhanded effort we'd put into trying to solve the problem. A simple, direct approach to such problems by parents and teachers can work wonders.

Even though this development of listening and speaking vocabularies is crucial, we have to be realistic about it. No one parent has the time or patience to listen to the endless stream of chatter that most kids can put out. When you're "talked out," you'll do best to let kids know that you just don't want to listen right now because you are feeling tired or are too busy. This is far better than gritting your teeth and listening out of some sense of duty, for children will sense your true response. If you have not been clear with them, they might conclude that their talking is dumb or boring or that you *never* want to hear them talk. They clam up and all that valuable verbalizing experience is lost.

Our modern nuclear family, with its absence of grandmas, grandpas, aunts, uncles, and other assorted relatives who could lend their ears to a child's practice conversation, puts a strain on modern parents. Nursery schools, day-care programs, play groups, trading baby-sitting, or any arrangement that puts kids in contact with other adults or kids and allows them more listening and talking interaction can be valuable in developing this verbal readiness for reading.

In the same vein, the teacher in the modern, overcrowded classroom doesn't have the time to listen to each and every child's practice verbalizing either. Yet it is important to find ways to provide kids with experiences that will stimulate their verbal abilities, build their vocabularies, and give them practice in communicating their thoughts and ideas in a logical manner.

Of course, children don't always need a responsive audience, one that will "talk back" to them. Sometimes a prop, something that will allow them to chatter away to no one in particular, is enough. For the individual child, a pet can be an attentive set of ears. If a real animal is not practical for your home or classroom, stuffed animals, miniature zoo animals with cages made from strawberry baskets, and the like make good substitutes. Children will chatter away for hours with their dolls. Families of little play people allow kids to act out all kinds of fantasies and develop their oral language skills as well.

Toy telephones, or better yet, real ones will also stimulate lots of verbalizing. A tape recorder easy enough for a child to operate by himself will also help develop those language skills. Recordings of children's books and fairy tales are available in many public libraries and will give kids the opportunity to listen and expand their vocabularies even though there is no adult around to read to them.

The much maligned TV set also plays an important role in developing a child's listening and speaking vocabularies. As teachers, we are well aware of the value of shows like "Sesame Street," "Electric Company," and "Mr. Rodgers." It's easy to spot kids who come to school having watched these shows at home. Their oral language skills—in fact, all readiness skills—are often more advanced. This effect can be more pronounced among children who have no siblings and thus less opportunity to develop these skills.

To develop oral language skills, kids need to do more than talk to themselves, listen to records, and watch television. They also need to learn to think and express themselves clearly and logically in order to communicate effectively with others.

Acting Out Fantasies

With groups of two or more children, there is an endless variety of ways to get them to sophisticate their oral language skills. We always keep a trunk full of costumes and dress-up clothes on hand to get kids to act out their fantasies as well as develop those skills. We've noticed that some little boys have already adopted such rigid sex roles that they are reluctant to put on dress-up clothes, which seem too girlish for them. We include lengths of material that can be draped into costumes. The cloth doesn't seem to have the same stigma for such kids. From time to time, we add special props like a toy stethoscope and a doctor's bag to the dress-up trunk. Not only does this add fuel to the fantasies and new words to the vocabularies, but it also helps kids deal with the fears they often have about visiting the doctor.

Puppets also stimulate this fantasy play. Sometimes a shy child will feel more comfortable talking with the help of a puppet. You can create very special puppets by taking an 8 by 10-inch (or

larger) photograph of the child and mounting it on a piece of cardboard. Then cut the child's body from the photo and tape a ruler to the back to create a handle for the puppet.

Acting out stories that have been read to them, playing house, retelling stories they've heard on records to each other, "reading" picture books to each other by telling what's happening in each of the pictures—all these activities are excellent. We also rely on the old standby, Show and Tell. In our classrooms, we call it "Sharing Time" which includes a bit more. Kids may share thoughts, feelings, dreams, fears, and personal problems as well as show something specific to the class. Parents can create this same kind of experience in the home, at family meetings or in more informal conversations.

Tell Me a Story

Another activity that will get kids talking with each other is a game using a simple deck of cards with pictures cut from maga-

zines pasted on them. Each player chooses a card at random from the deck and then tells a story about the picture he has chosen. If a child has trouble, you can help by asking questions like "What does the picture remind you of?" and "Have you ever seen or used one of these or been to a place like this?"

Good Vibes

One game that works well with a group, but could be played in a family setting, is one our kids call "Good Vibes." The kids sit in a circle on the floor and one child sits in the center. Then we go around the circle and each kid says something he likes about the child in the center. The comments may range from "I like Sally because she always shares her toys with me" to "I like the Snoopy socks you are wearing." Incidentally, this game can work wonders for the kid who is having a hard time and is "acting out" in the classroom or around the house that day.

Describing Games

Sometimes we structure the kids' verbalizing activities in order to get them to expand their vocabularies and be precise in their use of language. For instance, we may take an object and pass it around the group and ask each kid to pick a word that describes or "tells about" the object, a word no one else has picked. Thus, a rock might be described as hard, solid, thick, cool, grayish, or spotted. This activity works well for a parent and child at home or for a couple of kids by themselves.

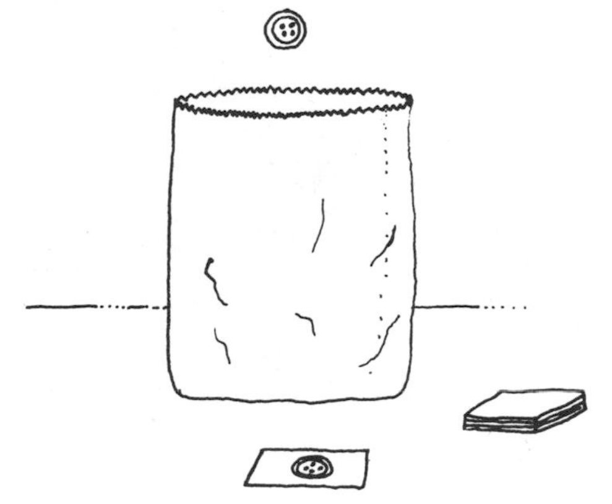

Still another activity that will increase kids' vocabularies is to have one describe a hidden object to another. The second kid then guesses the object. It helps if the kid who is describing the object actually has the object hidden in his hand, or perhaps inside a bag, so that the other child can't see it. Sometimes, with very young children, we make a more formal game of this with a set of objects, such as buttons, thimbles, paper clips, toy cars, rolls of tape, etc., inside bags and a matching set of picture cards. The child reaches in the bag, feels the object, and describes it to the other one without actually naming the object. The second child selects the picture that best matches the description. Playing this game with an adult or an older child will really stretch the younger one's vocabulary.

Giving Directions

To teach skill in giving directions, we have one kid blindfold another and lead him around with verbal instructions. Another way of getting kids to make their language specific and clear is to give each kid a pile of blocks. Place a barrier between them so they can't see each other. Then one child builds a structure from his pile of blocks. As he adds each block, he gives verbal instructions to the other child describing what he's doing. That child tries to build the same structure, according to directions. When the barrier is removed, kids often get fascinated in dissecting what went wrong and who misunderstood whom.

The Connection between School and Home

As we mentioned earlier, many kids are real chatterboxes. It's just a matter of having the time to listen and of stimulating them to stretch their oral and listening vocabularies. Other children who are quite verbal at home will be shy and reticent at school. The gap between school and home is scary for them. Sometimes, parents and teachers can help make the connection between home and school more secure for these children by visiting back and forth. This has been particularly effective in our preschool classes, where many of the children are venturing out on their own for the first time. A mom or dad who shows up and spends some time in the classroom can help reassure the child that school, too, is a safe part of his world. Likewise, a teacher who can visit the shy or reticent child's home will do a lot to reassure the child about the school environment. Of course, this is not always possible and it is, perhaps, unfair to ask a teacher who already gives so much, generally for so little (in terms of pay), to spend nonworking hours in this way. However, we have found other ways for teachers to strengthen the connection between home and school without visiting. For instance, once or twice a year, we hold a Teddy Bear Convention. Somehow, dragging your beloved security symbol along with you makes school a bit less frightening and opens up the more reticent kids.

We have always taught in private schools, which allow us a bit more freedom. Thus, in the first few months, we always have a sleep-over in the classroom. The kids bring their teddy bears, sleeping bags, and usually their parents. We spend a great deal of class time preparing a completely tasteless menu of hot dogs, carrot sticks, and marshmallows. Then we pop popcorn, tell ghost stories, and generally have a wonderful time. After this event, many of our formerly shy children open up and become more verbal in class.

Another way in which we try to make our classrooms conducive to children's verbalizing is to simply be quiet ourselves. Too many times we adults do all the talking for children. They don't have a chance to get a word in edgewise. Without being obvious about it, take a half hour or so and limit your talking to yes and no and one-syllable words as much as possible. You'll be amazed at how much talking the kids will do and how easy it is for you as an adult to fall out of the habit of doing all of the talking.

Since we do not run traditional classrooms with rows of desks filled with silent children, our classrooms are not always the most quiet or tranquil of places. They are filled with the life of children and its inevitable noise. Still, we try to make "quiet spaces," lofts filled with pillows and such, where the possibility for quiet conversation exists. For some reticent children who are too shy to force their voices above the din, these quiet places and class quiet times where only whispering is allowed are important. Another way in which we make our classrooms conducive to quiet talk is to send some or all of the children to different points around the school to simply sit quietly by themselves for a while. When they return to the classroom, we all sit together and talk about what we saw and felt during our quiet time. The tranquility this brings to the classroom atmosphere not only astounds us each time, but seems to create an environment in which the quieter child feels comfortable talking.

Nonverbal Communication

Sometimes, despite all our efforts, we have come across children who have so little verbal skill or are so afraid that rarely do we hear a sound out of them. These children need special help. With such kids, we usually start with nonverbal and subverbal communication. For instance, we might ask such a child to play at what we call "the messy table." The messy table is filled with Play-doh, mud, Rice Krispies, Fizzies, or Slime (a commercial toy that is an indescribably yucky, green, slimy material). After they've played at the table for a while (these silent ones are the most obedient of children, always doing exactly what they're told), we ask them to tell us with sounds how the various materials feel. As they squish and crackle at us, we supply the words, "Oh, the Slime feels squishy, the cereal crackles."

We also encourage these quiet ones in other nonverbal ways of communicating. Simple musical instruments of the clang and bang variety are excellent for this purpose. Kazoos work well, too. For a little boy in one of our classes, it was literally his instrument of liberation. First he replaced his constantly in-the-mouth thumb with a kazoo. After a while, he began to "talk" to the other children through the kazoo. At first, it was simple yes and no replies tooted through the kazoo. Then he ventured longer answers and finally asked questions—still tooting through the kazoo. As he was drawn more and more into the group and class activities, talking through the kazoo became increasingly impractical, and in time he abandoned it altogether.

We try to involve these reticent children in regular class activities, in ways that are not threatening to them. In class plays, they get to be "the princess who couldn't talk," or the animal whose only speaking part is a bark, meow, or cluck. There is also the "villain theory," which we fall back on from time to time. Encouraging quiet kids to play the "bad guy," to become the epitome of evil, seems to loosen language blocks. After all, if you are the incarnation of nastiness, what's left to be afraid of?

Pantomimes, pretending to be a mirror and following another's movements, acting out assigned roles like being a Raggedy Ann doll, a candle in the wind, a motorcycle roaring, a flower growing—all of these nonverbal communications are the necessary first steps for these children.

Kids who have a rich background in oral language, who've had plenty of opportunities to talk with others, roll new words around their tongues, and practice communication skills, are well prepared for reading. As parents and teachers, we can create environments that will help kids develop these important skills.

Concept Development

Another area closely related to reading to children and helping them develop their speaking and listening vocabularies is concept development. Jean Piaget, the well-known child psychologist, tells a story about a little boy who couldn't learn to read the word *night*. He was put to bed every night in a room with Venetian blinds and an air conditioner cutting out all the velvety darkness and sleepy sounds of the night. He had never experienced moonlight or star glow. He had no background of meaningful experience and therefore could not learn the verbal symbol *night* which represented all of this.

Learning to read is more than merely recognizing the written symbols that stand for speech; it is the process of gaining meaning from those symbols. A child must have a mental image or concept to go with the printed symbols or he will not be able to read. Concept development is not an isolated skill, but an accumulation of images and understandings that a child pieces together from his background of experience.

Experiential Background

Presenting children with a wide variety of experiences—visits to the fire station and museums, chances to paint and draw, trips to the movies and puppet shows, opportunities to listen to and to make music, chances to put on plays or to play house—also helps get them ready for reading. A rich background of experience increases a child's vocabulary and understanding of the world and provides him with the opportunity to develop his concept of the world.

Here again, preschool programs, nursery schools, or some sort of child-care arrangement with other families can be helpful. Such arrangements will mean that kids can have more opportunities for new experiences than any one family could ever provide.

Take advantage of the resources in your community. Fire stations are usually delighted to arrange tours. The grocer will often be glad to let you behind the scenes in the market. The junkyard, the post office, a factory, or any community enterprise will probably be open to letting a bunch of kids in for a behind-the-scenes tour. Even a simple walk through town can be valuable.

Sometimes we have organized our classrooms around what we call "tender topics" themes. A visit to the doctor or dentist when you're not actually sick can be an important thing for young children who usually encounter the doctor or dentist for the first time when they are sick, scared, and in need of treatment. We've visited veterinarians' offices, old folks' homes, and centers for the handicapped after having read books, watched films, and talked about these things in the classroom beforehand.

We also organize our classrooms around a central theme and then plan dozens of activities related to this theme. Parents can do the same thing by selecting a theme and exploring it through all sorts of projects. For instance, at one point, we decided to study fish. We read books and stories about fish, made fish puppets, went fishing, dissected fish, made up plays about fish, created an aquarium, visited a pet store that specialized in fish, invited an ichthyologist to class, painted pictures of fish, made fish windsocks, drew a life-size portrait of a thirty-foot whale shark, used fish to fertilize our gardens, toured a government fish hatchery, and wrote letters to the President protesting the treatment of ocean-dwelling creatures like whales and dolphins. Our children had, to say the least, a thorough experience with fish. You needn't, of course, be so elaborate, but the opportunity to explore an experience from many different angles and points of view is all part of helping a child to develop his concept of the world.

Symbolizing

Another part of forming concepts and being ready to read is the ability to understand and use symbols. Printed words are just symbols for spoken sounds. The spoken sounds are also symbols. The sound of the letters *m-a-m-a* is a symbol for mother. The notion that one thing can stand for another or represent something else is a learned notion. Babies begin this complex learning process in their cribs. As they grow older, children use their imaginations and imitative play in developing their ability to use symbols. Thus, a child who uses a corncob as a doll or leaves and twigs for paper and pencil in playing school is experimenting with the use of symbols. The process of understanding and using symbols is a complex one that takes place in various stages. If you show a very young child a picture or photograph of his father and say, "That's Daddy," he'll probably look at you like you're crazy. Daddy is a three-dimensional human being, not a two-dimensional image (though it's not likely your average two-year-old will put it in quite these terms). It is not until later, when he brings you a page of scribbles and proudly announces, "That's Daddy," that he has begun to master the process of symbolizing.

Parents and teachers can aid children in the development of understanding symbols by providing lots of opportunities for imitative play. A housekeeping corner with an orange-crate stove, a refrigerator, and sink invites kids to engage in imitative play. A trunkful of costumes and props with firefighters' hats, clown ruffles, high heels, stethoscopes, and similar props encourages the kind of acting-out play that is the basis of symbolizing.

Sometimes we ask kids to create a certain kind of play space. For instance, once we suggested to a group of kids that they make a dentist's office. By the time they were finished, they had every tool they needed, including a plumber's wrench, a hacksaw, and assorted pliers—a veritable torture chamber of horrors, but they had fun, acted out fears, and participated in the kind of imitative play that helps them to learn about symbols and to develop concepts.

One symbol-forming game that we enjoy playing with kids is shield making. This game is based on an Indian ritual. Certain Indian tribes had a puberty rite in which a young boy went alone into the wilderness for a few days. When he returned, he would report to the tribal elders the thoughts and experiences he had during his vigil. Based on what the boy said, the shield maker would design a personal shield for the boy. Through the use of Indian symbols, the shield would reveal his personality, his strengths and weaknesses, and the path that the young man needed to take on his journey to fullness in this life.

Our shield making doesn't involve as much ritual, and certainly not as much wisdom. Still, making shields is a way of talking in symbols about yourself. We give our children blank shields like the one pictured on the next page and ask them to draw pictures in each of the four sections of the shield.

In the shield pictured here, the drawing in the upper left-hand corner of the shield pictures a little girl living inside a tree trunk and was drawn in response to the question "What's something

HOLLY

you would like to do but have never been able to do?" The drawing in the upper right-hand corner was drawn in response to the question "What was your scariest dream?" and shows a devil chasing her at night. The question for the lower left-hand corner was "What's something you wished everybody believed in?" This child wished that everyone believed she had a swimming pool in her backyard with flowers all around it. The question for the last section was "Who would you like for a secret invisible playmate?" Her answer was that she'd like to have ten million kids for invisible playmates who'd go out and explore the world ("But," she added, "they'd have to stay together—I don't want ten million kids getting lost!").

These are just sample questions. You can use almost anything: hopes, fears, dreams, wishes. This exercise draws a lot from kids. It's a vehicle for developing vocabulary, verbalizing thoughts and feelings, and using symbols. And, because it draws on the inner feelings of the child, it promotes his first steps in learning to creatively express himself.

The ideas and suggestions in this section will help to acquaint kids with books, to develop their oral language, and to provide a rich background of exercises that will allow children to develop their concepts of the world and to understand symbols.

You may find that most of these opportunities are already a natural part of your children's day-to-day activities. If not, make the extra effort to incorporate some of these things into their lives, for the effort will pay off as they begin to learn to read.

3

OFF TO A GOOD START: VISION AND HEARING

Reading is both a visual and an auditory process. Kids have to be able to see clearly in order to be able to distinguish the letters of a word and to hear clearly in order to distinguish spoken sounds. This is not to say that children with impaired vision or hearing cannot learn to read. In fact, researchers are not at all clear about the relationship between visual and auditory abilities and reading achievement. There are many children with visual or auditory problems who are excellent readers. Yet for others these sorts of problems, if they are not treated, will lead to reading difficulties. Many such children will "turn off" to reading, choosing some other activity that is easier for them.

Checking Vision

Alert parents and teachers can often spot visual problems. A number of educational researchers have tried to identify the kinds of symptoms that characterize children with vision problems. The following list of symptoms is derived from their work:

- facial contortions, especially squinting
- tenseness during visual work
- holding books close to the face
- tilting the head
- thrusting the head forward
- body tenseness when looking at distant objects
- moving the head excessively while looking at books or doing close work
- rubbing eyes frequently
- tending to avoid close visual work

- slanting books or other materials at an angle to see them
- excessive blinking

Most children exhibit some of these signs occasionally, but if two or more of these symptoms persist, a child is more likely to need visual care and should be seen by a physician. Also, children who are given reading material with print that is too small may exhibit some of these signs. At birth, the eye is only one-third of its adult size. This prevents precise focus of the image of near objects on the retina. As the eyeball lengthens, farsightedness decreases and the child is able to focus clearly at close range. Studies indicate that many children do not achieve the ablility to focus at close range on very tiny objects until about the age of eight. Thus, most books for children are printed in an oversized typeface. If your child exhibits some of the behaviors associated with eye strain, first check to see that the print in the books and reading materials he is using are printed in oversized typeface.

This size and style of type is suitable for primary readers.

In addition to watching out for the kinds of behaviors mentioned in this list, the games and activities described below can help parents and teachers spot kids with visual problems.

String Game

This exercise, which we call the String Game, helps us check close-range focusing power. It requires a certain amount of control of the eye muscles to focus on an object that is close at hand. Some children, even though they don't have a real vision problem that requires medical attention, will not yet have developed very good control of those muscles. They may tend to shy away from close work or tire easily. This exercise helps us to recognize their problem, and practicing it can help them strengthen and develop control over those muscles.

More rarely, this exercise will turn up a child with a lazy eye. We all have one eye that is stronger than the other, but for some children the discrepancy between the eyes is quite pronounced. They begin to rely more and more on the stronger eye. A typical behavior for such kids is holding books at an angle to suit the strong eye. The more they rely on the good eye, the more the vision in the other eye deteriorates, and this, of course, can lead to more serious vision problems.

For this exercise, you will need a piece of string about the same length as the distance between the child's elbow and knuckles. Tie a knot in the string about where the wrist would be. Ask the child to hold one end of the string against his nose and to stretch the string out in front, level with the nose as shown here.

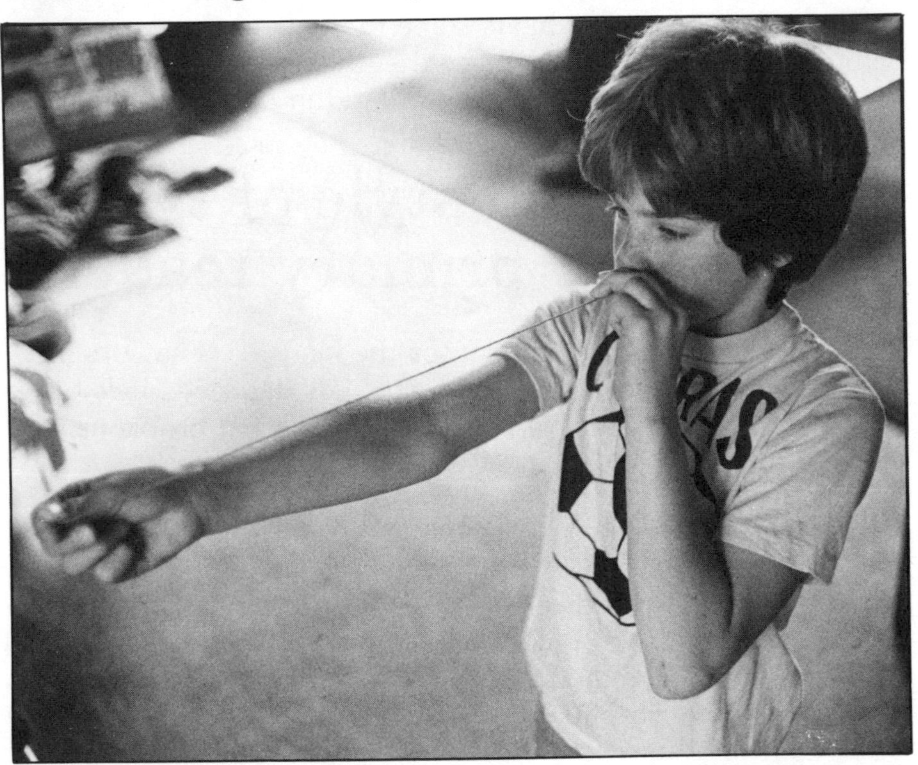

Then ask the child to look at the knot. The knot should be clear and bright and in focus. The child should see double strings that converge on the knot. Right behind the knot the child should again see double strings. In other words, the child should see an X of strings. The point where the lines of the X cross should be exactly on the knot, as shown here. Have the child check the place where the double vision strings are clear and bright. If one string fades in and out, this may indicate that the child is not using one eye. He may therefore be erasing much of what he sees. This could lead to serious eye problems as the lazy eye gets weaker and weaker.

Of course, there is a natural amount of fading because everyone tends to use one eye more than the other. Also, the eyes will tend to slip and lose clear focus even in people with perfect vision. However, if after playing this game for a while you suspect something is amiss, don't hesitate to have the child tested by an expert.

Tongue Depressor Exercise

Another problem that can affect reading is weak inner eye muscles. Here again, this does not mean that the child has a problem requiring medical attention. It may be that he just needs to strengthen these muscles. A child with this problem will not be able to focus for any prolonged length of time without feeling eyestrain. We use an exercise that indicates the strength of these eye muscles and can also be used to strengthen weak muscles.

For this exercise, we use a tongue depressor with an X drawn on the top as shown here. The child holds the tongue depressor at arm's length. The idea is to bring the tongue depressor to the tip of the nose, crossing the eyes so that the X remains a single image. (see illustration on p. 42). The child should be able to hold the image for a count of ten and, if possible, a count of twenty. The tendency is for the eyes to shift and the image to split into double vision. Some people experience no difficulty in reading even though they cannot hold the image for the count of twenty. However, many people, both adults and children, who experience blurring or strain while reading will benefit from repeating this exercise a few times each day and strengthening the inner eye muscles.

Checking Hearing

Adequate hearing is also important to reading. Obviously, a kid who cannot hear well is going to have problems learning to read, especially with phonics or the sounding out of words. Children who have a physical hearing loss are likely to have speech problems because most auditory deficiencies involve high-frequency sounds. Since most consonants are high-frequency, a child with a hearing loss will usually have trouble pronouncing and recognizing these sounds.

The following list of symptoms are often exhibited by children with hearing difficulties:

- difficulty in hearing and pronouncing consonant sounds
- tilting the head when spoken to
- body tenseness when listening to faraway sounds
- cupping the ears with the hands to hear

Here again, many young children will exhibit one or more of these symptoms from time to time even though there is nothing amiss. Most young children have difficulty pronouncing certain consonants, expecially the letter *r*. However, if you notice the symptoms described in the list and your instinct tells you that something is wrong, have the child tested further by an expert. We also have three simple exercises or games parents and teachers can use to help them identify kids who might have hearing problems.

Whisper Test

The Whisper Test has long been used by teachers and other nonexperts to screen kids for problems. It should be done in a room of normal dimensions (that is, not outdoors or in a gymnasium). The child stands about twenty feet away from you with one ear turned toward you. The child is instructed not to look at you, but to repeat the words he hears. You say words in a low voice, and the child repeats them. If necessary, move closer until his responses are correct. The other ear is tested in the same way.

If the child hesitates, strains to hear, turns to look at you, or cannot hear the instructions, he should be tested further. Obviously, this test is not highly accurate. The loudness of your whisper and the acoustics of the room will affect the results of the test, but it can give a rough indication. The following test will also help you gauge a child's auditory acuity.

Watch-Tick Test

Any loud-ticking watch (we use an Ingersoll or Westclox Pocket Ben) can be used for the Watch-Tick Test. A child with normal hearing will be able to hear such a watch at a distance of about forty-eight inches. Testing is done in a quiet room. The child stands with one ear toward you and puts his finger in the other ear. Hold a card beside the child's head so he cannot see the watch. First, hold the watch near the child's ear and gradually move it farther away until the child can no longer hear the watch. Record the distance at which the sound disappears. Then, hold the watch at a distance of forty-eight or more inches from the child's ear. Gradually move it toward his ear. Note the distance at which the first tick is heard. Add the two distances together and divide by two. If your answer is less than twenty, the child requires further testing by an expert. The other ear is tested in the same manner.

Follow the Sound

Here is another game that should be done indoors. We ask all the kids to close their eyes and follow the sound of our voice with their noses as we move around the room. As we move from location to location, we gradually lower our voices to the slightest whisper. Children who seem confused by this exercise, who are out of phase with our movements or move their heads around in a bewildered, searching fashion, should be tested further by a specialist.

We also play this same game using an autoharp, sounding low, medium, and high pitches as we move about the room. A child who has a hearing loss at a specific frequency will not be able to follow the sound and will be confused by this exercise. Again, such a child should be tested by a hearing specialist.

Obviously these simple visual and auditory tests are not perfectly accurate. They cannot detect children with subtle deficiencies. They are not meant to take the place of regular examinations by a specialist, but they can help alert parents and teachers to the need for further testing. Besides, to the kids they are not tests, but games, and they enjoy them.

Perception

Being ready to read involves more than just a pair of healthy ears and eyes. The brain must also be able to interpret the information gathered by the eyes and ears correctly. It is important to recognize the difference between a child who cannot hear a word and a child who cannot discriminate between sounds. The first child has a hearing loss, which is a physical problem; the second child has an auditory perception problem. In this case, the brain is not accurately interpreting the messages that the ears are sending it. Such children may not "hear" the difference between words like *pin* and *pen*. Similarly, the messages that the eyes send to the brain may not be received accurately. Children having visual perception problems will tend to reverse letters like *b* and *d* or even entire words, reading *was* for *saw*. Some of these children have "word blindness." Such children will simply not "see" certain words or even entire lines of print.

No one is entirely certain what causes these perception problems. Some experts feel it is a hereditary problem. Others blame minimal brain damage. Still others feel that perceptual problems are rooted in emotional problems. Sometimes it is merely a case of slow development. These reversal and discrimination problems are common to all young children. Most kids outgrow them by the age of eight or nine. If you are playing some of the perceptual games and activities described below with the children and find a child who is having a lot of difficulty, don't panic. Chances are his perceptual skills are simply taking longer to develop than other kids'. Playing these games may even remedy his problems. However, if your intuition tells you that something is amiss, you might take that child to a learning disability center or a perceptual development expert for evaluation. The best place to find help is through a pediatrician. Also, many colleges and universities have special programs to evaluate and help children with perceptual difficulties. Call your local college or university and ask to speak to someone in the education department. Explain your concern to him and ask him to recommend a center for testing.

It is important for you to know that because a child has perceptual problems, this does not mean that a child is unintelligent. The term "minimal brain damage" sounds scary to most parents and conjures up associations with mental retardation, but please don't be frightened by the terminology. "Minimal brain damage" or "perceptual handicap" does not mean impaired intelligence. Before we recognized perceptual difficulties for what they were and developed special teaching methods to deal with them, such children were labeled "slow" or "dumb." After all, they couldn't learn to read so they must be pretty stupid, right? Wrong. Don't let groundless fears about what you might discover keep you from seeking help. Children with perceptual difficulties will need special help in learning to read.

There are many different types of visual and auditory perception skills that are important in learning to read. Most children develop these skills quite naturally through their play. It is silly, perhaps even harmful, to interrupt a child's normal play impulses and impose a "perceptual skills development curriculum" on him. But parents and teachers who are aware of the kinds of perceptual abilities involved in learning to read can make sure that their children have an environment rich in opportunities to develop those skills. The following pages describe some of the perceptual abilities that are involved in reading. The games and activities described are ones that we've found valuable and that kids seem to enjoy. Many teachers use these and similar activities in their classes. Parents will find that many of these same activities can be used in the home either by the child on his own or with the parent, or in some cases, with a group of friends.

Figure/Ground Perception

One perceptual phenomenon that is closely linked to reading readiness is figure/ground perception. The image shown here is a rather well-known example of this phenomenon.

Some people looking at this image will see two profiles. Others will see a vase. If you see a vase, then the white vase is in your perceptual foreground and the black area has receded into your perceptual background. This ability to make what we see on a two-dimensional surface into a three-dimensional image allows us to make visual sense of what we are seeing. This figure/ground perceptual ability is important in learning to read because it enables us to glean letters from the background of a printed page; otherwise, a page of print is merely a bunch of meaningless black splotches on a white page.

We are so accustomed to dealing with print and figure/ground perception that it is hard for most of us grownups to understand how meaningless print can look to the untrained eye of the child. Perhaps the image pictured here will help you get a sense of how a child first sees printed matter. The image is a very difficult one for most people to identify. Even after they have been told that it is a photographer kneeling and using a Graflex camera, many people still cannot "see" it or make visual sense of the image. Children have the same kind of visual confusion when they first confront printed matter. It takes familiarity with letter forms and skill in perceiving figure/ground relationships before a child can make visual sense out of a page of print.

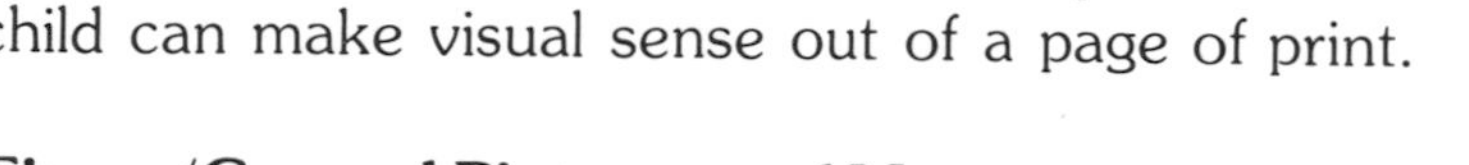

Figure/Ground Pictures and Mazes

Games like the ones pictured here help kids develop the ability to perceive figure/ground relationships. If a child has trouble with these exercises, you might devise some more, perhaps starting with some simpler ones and working up to more complex ones. Inexpensive books with these kinds of figure/ground per-

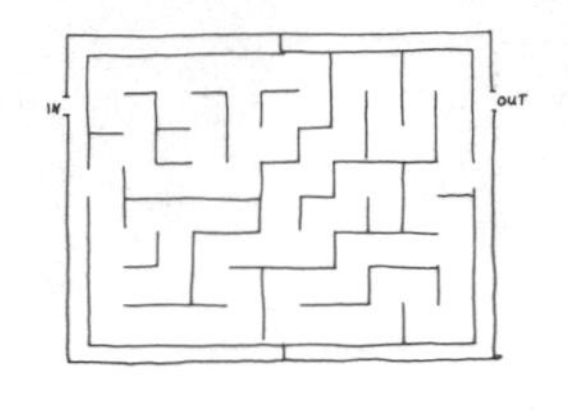

ception games are usually available in supermarkets and drugstores. "Sesame Street" episodes often include such figure/ground games. The inexpensive Sesame Street magazines and workbooks are also a good source for these kinds of exercises.

Drawing Game

We have another game that helps refine figure/ground perceptual skills. To start, one person draws a simple scribble or image on a sheet of paper. The sheet is then passed on to the next player, who must add to the picture and change it into something else. Then the next player does the same, and the next, and so on. In playing this game, the child is shifting the figure/ground relationships in the drawing until he can glean a new image and add some lines that will bring that image into the perceptual foreground.

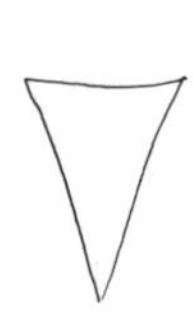

Cloud Watching

Sometimes we go cloud watching. We all lie on the ground with our heads forming a circle. We watch the clouds float by and exercise our figure/ground perception skills by "seeing" various

shapes and forms in the clouds. Of course, most people don't know we're doing such important work. They think we're just having fun. And, we are.

Listening Game

The ability to perceive foreground and background applies to auditory as well as visual perception. Children need to be able to select one noise from the sea of sounds that surrounds us and focus on it. Some children have difficulty doing this. They react to all stimuli equally. Parents and teachers may complain that such children "don't listen" or "won't pay attention." Actually, they are paying too much attention. They cannot narrow the focus of their attention and pay attention to a single sound.

We use an exercise developed by Maria Montessori to help kids refine their ability to bring one sound into their perceptual foreground and focus on that sound. We ask the kids to sit or lie down comfortably and be completely quiet. After they can do this for a few minutes (no easy task for many children), we ask them to listen for the most faraway sound they can hear. Sometimes we go around the group asking each child to report quietly on the sound he is hearing. Can the others hear the same sound? Then we might ask them to notice the closest sound, the loudest, the softest, and so on—anything, so long as they are focusing on a single sound out of the general background of noise around us. Parents may find that bedtime or naptime is a particularly good moment for trying this exercise.

Hunter/Hunted

This game is a favorite in our classrooms. The children form a circle about twelve feet in diameter. One child is the hunter and another is the hunted. They stand opposite each other within the circle, and the hunter is blindfolded. The children forming the circle have to be very quiet, so the hunter will not be unduly distracted by extraneous noises. We usually start this game by sitting quietly in a circle. We whisper while explaining the rules and choosing the players. This helps set the quiet tone for the game. The object of the game is for the hunted to tiptoe across the circle (one step, then a pause) until he reaches a designated player on the opposite side of the circle without, of course, being caught by the hunter.

The children forming the circle guard the hunter and hunted so no one gets hurt—a very gentle touch will tell the hunter if he is too close to the edge. The hunter must make all other noises recede and bring the soft tiptoe sounds of the hunted into his perceptual foreground in order to catch his prey.

Perceptual Consistency

Another perceptual phenomenon that is important in learning to read is perceptual consistency. Consistency in perception depends upon the ability to generalize so that we can recognize something as being the same even though we see it in another

context. For example, when we look at an object, say a vase of flowers, it looks different, depending on the angle from which we see it. The actual image that is sent through our eyes to the brain differs depending on whether we see the vase from the side, above, or below. As these photographs illustrate, we are actually seeing three distinct images. The human brain has a wonderful mechanism that allows us to perceive these different images as one thing—a vase of flowers. A child needs a well-developed sense of perceptual consistency so he can recognize that a word in a different book or on a different page or in a different style or size of type is still the same word. Thus, he will be able to recognize the word GOOD as being the same as the word *good.*

Shape Walk

One game we play that involves perceptual consistency is something we call the Shape Walk. It can be played with an individual or a whole group of children. You start by cutting some simple geometric shapes—squares, circles, triangles. Then go for a walk and ask the kids to find these shapes in the buildings, trees, plants, or whatever they see as they walk. By identifying a circle with the top of a tree stump, children are developing their ability to generalize and to recognize forms in different contexts.

Find the Shape

Another exercise that involves perceptual consistency is asking kids to find simple shapes in a drawing. You can make these simple drawings yourself, or look in supermarkets or drug-stores for inexpensive activity books that contain these sorts of exercises.

Discrimination

Still another perceptual skill involved in reading is the ability to discriminate, or to perceive differences. Many letters of the alphabet are very similar. The letters *b* and *d*, for instance, are just reversals of each other. Many of the words we hear sound almost exactly the same (*pin*, *pen*). Being ready to read involves the ability to perceive these rather minute differences that distinguish one letter from another or one sound from another, which requires finely tuned powers of visual and auditory discrimination.

We begin to tune our perceptual discrimination abilities in the crib. If we don't close ourselves off, we continue to tune them all our lives. If we can find a quiet place within ourselves and turn off all the worries, problems, anticipations, fears, and dreams that are usually clanging and banging about our brains, we can clear

our perceptual fields. Then we can focus our attention and truly "see," perceive clearly, what is before us. Most children have an amazing ability to do this (perhaps because they've got less clanging and banging in their brains). We grownups often forget about this amazing ability that children have. Many times when we see children lying or sitting quietly staring vacantly at something, we tend to think they're "doing nothing." But the child who is lying on his back idly, watching the clouds move by, is probably hard at work refining his visual discrimination skills. The child lazing in the afternoon sun examining two blades of grass between her fingers is noticing very minute and precise differences. She is tuning her powers of visual discrimination at a very subtle and precise level.

In comparison, the bright (often garish) and slick toys, games, and apparatuses used by so many developmental specialists and early childhood curriculum experts to foster and develop discrimination skills seem rather crude. Parents and teachers would probably do better to join the children on the lawn, sprawling right alongside of them. Bringing the infinite shades of green in the lawn to the child's attention is a much more sophisticated exercise in visual discrimination than sorting bright blue, red, and yellow poker chips into piles according to color. This doesn't mean that sorting and matching activities are not of value. Any activity that requires a child to sort, to match, to categorize, to classify, or to judge whether things are the same or different, either visually or auditorily, will help to develop his perceptual discrimination powers. But there is no need to create a whole program or rigid curriculum of such activities.

Household Matching and Sorting

Opportunities to practice matching and sorting skills crop up all the time. Kids can help match pairs of socks, sort the laundry into piles according to color, set the table, and the like. There are any number of common household objects that can be used to help kids develop their visual discrimination abilities. A pile of but-

tons and an empty egg carton can be used for sorting. Ask kids to sort the buttons by size (big ones, little ones), color, shape, the number of holes in the center, the ones they like best, least, and so on. Pots and pans or an assortment of empty jars and other containers with lids will not only keep kids occupied, but will help them develop their matching skills as they try to fit the lids to the proper containers.

Card Games

Card games, which most children love, are also excellent for the matching and sorting abilities that develop visual discrimination. Crazy Eights is a great favorite. Each player is dealt eight cards, and the remaining cards are placed in a pile face down on the floor. The first card is turned face up and laid next to the other cards. The first player must play a card of the same suit (heart, club, spade, diamond) or the same number (ace, 2, 3, 4, 5, 6, 7, 8, 9, 10, jack, queen, king). If he has an 8, he may lay that on the pile and call any suit he chooses. The next player must then play a card from that suit. If a player doesn't have a card of the same suit, same number, or an 8, he must pick from the pile of face-down cards until he finds a card he can play. The first player to get rid of all his cards wins.

Go Fish is another favorite. Each player is dealt seven cards. The remaining cards are spread out on the floor, face down. The object is to get rid of all your cards. A player can get rid of his cards by laying down three or four cards of the same number. If only three are laid down, anyone can "play" on the three of a kind by laying down the fourth.

To start, the first player asks one of the other players for a card. For instance, he might say, "Do you have a two?" If the other player has the card, he passes it over and the first player gets to ask again. If not, then the first player has to "go fish" from the pile of face-down cards. If he picks up the card he has requested, he gets to ask the other players for another card. If not, he loses his turn and the next player gets to ask for a card. The winner is the first one to get rid of all his cards, the player who has laid down the most cards (minus the ones still in hand), or the player who has accumulated the most points (aces = 15 points, face cards = 10 points, all others = 5 points).

Any games that require kids to sort the cards in their hands according to suit or number and to match up pairs are excellent for developing visual perception skills.

Sorting Parts

Another sorting activity that kids particularly enjoy involves taking apart an old appliance like a clock or a radio. We give them egg cartons into which they sort all the little pieces of the appliance according to their own criteria. For instance, a child might sort the innards of a clock by categories like these: round parts with and without notches, round parts with teeth, round parts with big holes in the center, round parts with little holes in the center, etc. You might ask the children to sort according to one criterion and then to re-sort according to another criterion.

Sorting Sounds

There are also sorting and matching activities that involve auditory discrimination. One that our kids like involves filling jars and glasses with different amounts of water. Once they've got a bunch of variously filled glass containers, they strike them with a spoon and listen to the various notes that are produced. Some-

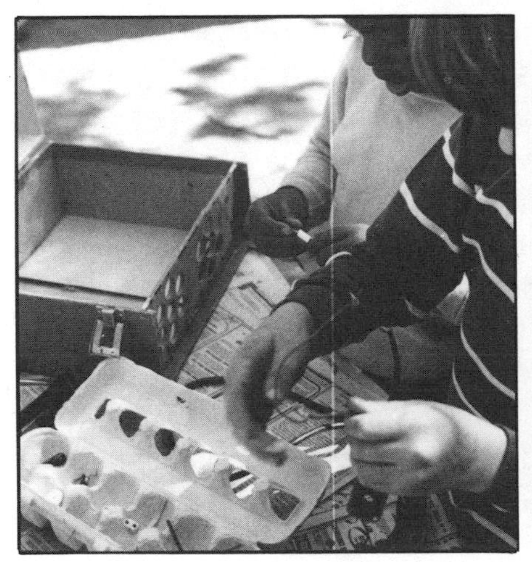

times they match up containers that produce the same or similar notes. Other times they sort the containers into some sort of order, perhaps starting with the lowest-sounding note and moving up to the highest-sounding note.

Matching Sounds

We usually make sets of sound containers for classroom use. Any matching set of opaque containers or jars, spray-painted so that the contents can't be seen, will do. We put a "noise-maker" (rice, paper clips, tacks, a liquid, bells) into each pair of jars. The idea of the game is for the children to match the jars that sound the same. We stick peel-off labels of the same color onto the bottom of the jars so the kids can check their matching.

Sound Collecting

If you have access to a simple cassette tape recorder, you can do a lot of auditory awareness exercises with kids. We make a tape of common sounds—water dripping, a refrigerator humming, a power saw droning, birds chirping, a car starting, a toilet flushing—and we ask the kids to identify them. Sometimes one or two kids go "sound collecting" and make a tape of sounds that they bring back for the others to identify. We have also made tapes of all the kids' voices and let them guess who was speaking. All of these activities require kids to perceive the differences in the sounds they hear. If we have a child whose auditory discrimination abilities are very immature, we let that child take the tape recorder home and make a tape for the rest of the kids to identify the next day. Kids are fascinated by the gadget, and these exercises force them to listen and to pay attention to what they are hearing.

Thump, Bump, Clunk, Ping

Kids seem to enjoy this one, especially the name. It can be played with one child or with a whole group. The child closes his eyes, and we drop various objects on the floor. For instance, we might drop a can, a pillow, a spoon, or a box and ask the child to guess what object we're dropping. Or we might drop one object, say a spoon, on the floor and ask the child to listen. Then we drop a whole series of objects on the floor and ask the child to tell us when he hears the same sound again. At first, we make it easy by dropping objects that make very different sounds. After the child has some success with this, we'll make it more difficult. Can you discriminate between the sound of a needle and a safety pin hitting the floor?

Visual-Motor Coordination

Another readiness skill linked to perceptual abilities is the ability to coordinate eye and hand movements. A child has to be able to coordinate his hand movements with what he sees in order to be able to write. He also has to coordinate the small muscles in his eyes in order to control eye movements from left to right across a page and from the end of one line of print to the beginning of another in order to read.

Most children learn to coordinate these movements quite naturally. A newborn child's movements in the crib are spasmodic and random. As they grow, babies learn to orient themselves in space. They develop a sense of sidedness which allows them to coordinate their muscle movements so that they can reach out and grasp things that they see. This sense of sideness or laterality develops as they become more adept at using their arms and hands. Eventually, they become so skilled that they can use the two sides of their bodies in opposition and begin to crawl.

As they learn to walk, skip, hop, jump, climb jungle gyms, and play catch, kids are continuing to refine their sense of sideness and their large muscle coordination. At the same time that they are developing this large muscle coordination, they are beginning to develop the small muscles in their hands and fingers. As they lace and tie their shoes and button their shirts, they are refining their control of these muscles and coordinating their visual perceptions with their motor control of these small muscles.

As large and small muscle coordination is developed, children also develop what psychologists call dominance. This means that they favor one side of their body over the other. For instance, in most children, the right side dominates. They use the right hand to paint, write, feed themselves, etc.; their right eye to peer through a microscope or telescope; their right foot to kick a ball. Of course, there are also many children whose left side predominates. Some rare children are ambidexterous; they can use either side of their body equally well. Some children have mixed dominance; they use the left hand, the right eye, the right foot, or some similar combination. Still others have a confused dominance. They never develop a clear dominance at all. They differ from ambidexterous children in that they don't use either side very well.

A clearly established dominance or laterality seems to be important in learning to read. Mixed dominance, as long as it is clearly and firmly established, does not seem to be a handicap; but children without a clearly established dominance have a great deal of difficulty in learning to read and often have other perceptual difficulties as well.

No one knows for sure what causes this failure to establish dominance. There are many theories and a great deal of debate about the subject. It may be physical or emotional. It may be that the child has not had a sufficient amount of experience exercising these large and small muscles to develop his dominance clearly. As we suggested earlier in talking about perceptual abilities in general, if you feel your child has a perceptual problem related to his sense of sideness, you would be wise to discuss the problem with your doctor or an educational consultant.

At any rate, we know that large and small muscle coordination, the ability to coordinate eye movements, and the sense of laterality or sideness are all important parts of being ready to read. Here again, parents and teachers who are aware of this importance can create an environment rich in opportunities and encourage activities that foster these abilities.

Large Muscle Coordination

Running, jumping, skipping, hopping, and games like tag, playing ball, and jumping rope are all important activities. Climbing trees, jungle gyms, or other climbing structures are also excellent for developing large muscle coordination and laterality.

If you don't have a backyard with trees, is there a park nearby? Unfortunately, jungle gyms and other pieces of climbing equipment are usually expensive. We've made some lovely climbing toys out of old tires. You can connect them in circular patterns, layer upon layer to form climbable heaps by drilling holes in the sides and bolting them together with 1½ by 5/16-inch bolts. (Don't forget to drill holes for rainwater drainage.)

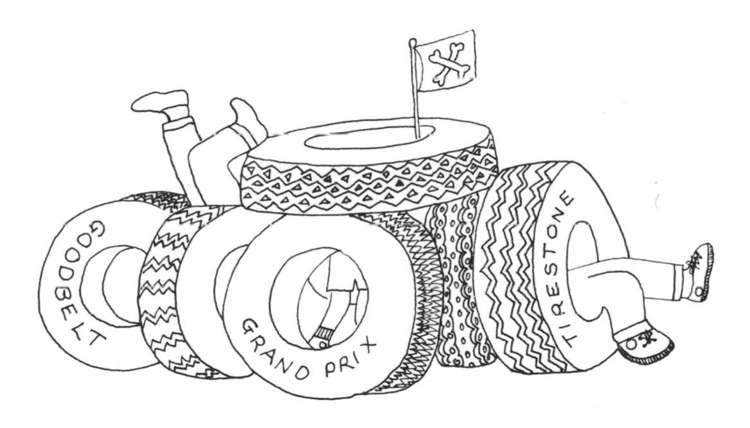

Balance Beam

We've found a simple balance beam to be a real aid in developing large muscle coordination. If you don't have trees, a park nearby, or room for a tire construction, it's an especially important piece of apparatus. It can be used indoors and it will exercise those large muscles, develop coordination, and refine a child's lateral sense.

All you'll need to make a balance beam is a two-by-four approximately ten feet long and three smaller two-by-fours, each approximately a foot and a half long. Cut notches in the smaller pieces to hold the beam. For very young children, or uncoordinated children, make the notches two inches deep and four inches wide so the two-by-four will lie flat. Once the children have become skilled at walking the beam, or for older children, cut the notches four inches deep and two inches wide so they'll be walking on the narrow edge of the two-by-four.

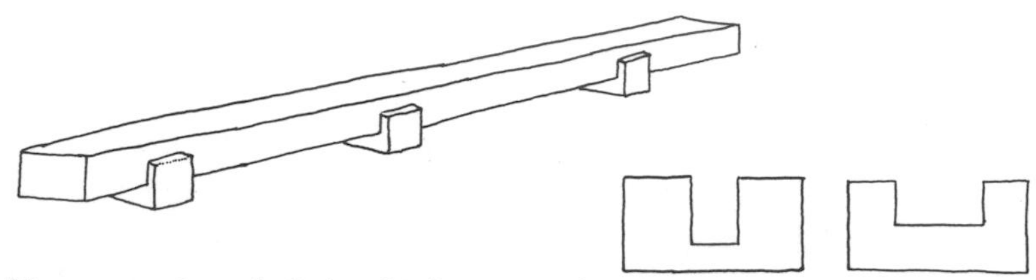

To start, just let the kids try walking from one end to another without falling off, or you might ask the kids to focus on a spot on the wall and walk across the beam with heel touching toe. Later on, they can practice walking backward, flapping their arms as they walk, or walking with their eyes closed.

Small Muscle and Eye-Hand Coordination

Cutting, sewing, pasting, scribbling, drawing, painting: all such activities will help kids to develop control of the small muscles in their hands and to coordinate eye and hand muscles. Hand and finger puppets are also excellent, and they'll stimulate oral language skills as well. Stringing beads or macaroni to make necklaces is another small-muscle activity kids enjoy. Encourage kids to dress themselves, lace their shoes, zip zippers, button buttons, and the like. This not only helps with small muscles, but gives them a new measure of independence from adults.

Sewing Cards

In the classroom, we use a set of homemade sewing and lacing boards that the kids enjoy. We cut a simple illustration from a magazine and paste it on to a sturdy piece of cardboard. For durability, we "laminate" it with a sheet of clear contact paper. Next we punch holes around the outer edges of the distinctive lines of the illustration. Then we tie a knot in one end of a long shoestring and ask the children to reproduce the design by lacing in and out of the holes with the shoestring.

Clothespin Drop

Another good one for eye-hand coordination is the old game of dropping clothespins through the neck of a bottle. With very young children, we use a plastic milk carton cut in the middle for a wider target. When they get skilled at this, we switch to the old-fashioned small-necked glass bottle.

Hardware Games

We also make a set of bolt, screw, and lock games that help kids exercise those tiny muscles in the hand. Because this involves tools and hardware that are usually only in the province of adults, most kids are fascinated by this game. A soda crate with a series of different little doors, each with a different bolt, is a real popular item. You can make a game by gluing the heads of various-sized bolts to a flat board with epoxy and letting the kids screw the proper nuts onto the bolt stems. Or, in a similar vein, drill a series of holes in a block of wood using drill bits of different diameters. Drill holes and let the kids use a screwdriver to twist a set of screws in and out of the holes.

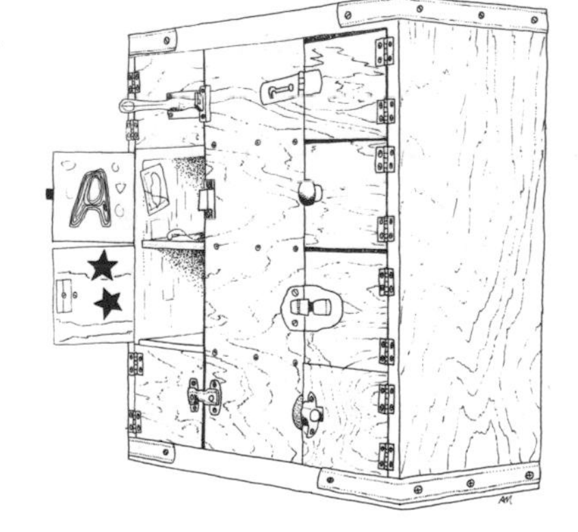

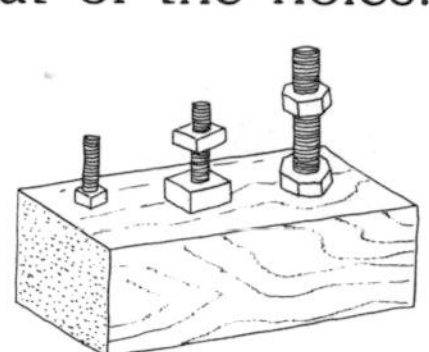

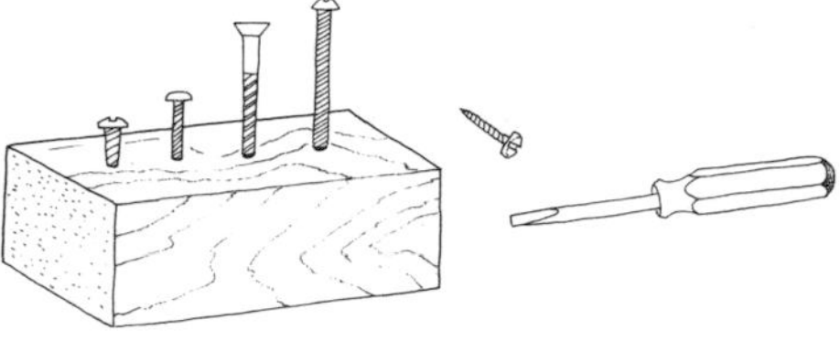

Labeling Drawings

As we mentioned earlier, scribbling, painting, and drawing are important preludes to writing. Even though it may not be immediately obvious to you, children's scribbles have a great deal of meaning. You can enter the child's world by asking what words might go with their pictures. Then you discover that (1) is a black apple, (2) a baseball man (umpire), (3) an artichoke upside down, and (4) a bird sleeping, flying—probably not what your grown-up

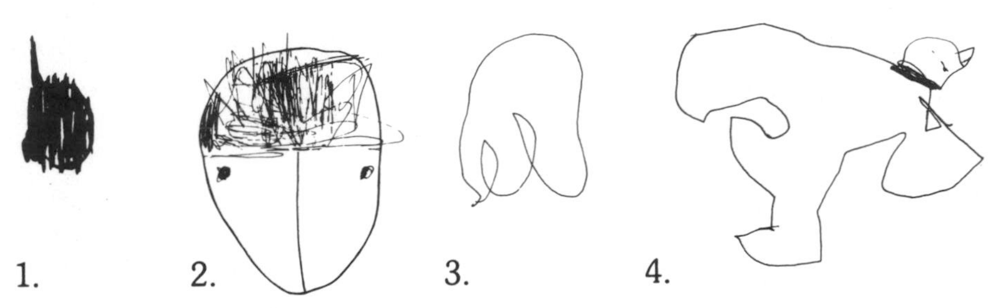

eyes could have seen without the help of the child's younger, fresher vision.

Label your children's drawings with titles of their own choosing. The attention will delight them and it is a good introduction to the method of teaching reading described in the next chapter.

Visual and Auditory Sequencing and Memory

Yet another readiness skill that is related to perception is visual and auditory sequencing and memory. Sounds and letters in words have a common sequence. Children have to be able to understand visual and auditory sequences and to be able to remember them in order to read.

As children read and talk about the stories they've been read, they are developing a sense of sequencing. One thing happens, and then another, and then another, as part of a logical series of events. Asking them questions like "What do you think will happen next?" as you're reading stories and books will help them grab hold of this concept of sequences.

On another level, they learn about sequencing as they gain experience in ordering things. For instance, they might line up all their cars and trucks in order from biggest to smallest, or a group of children might order themselves from shortest to tallest, youngest to oldest.

The games and activities described below are some of the exercises we've used with our kids to help develop their ability to understand sequencing and to recall or remember those sequences.

Cylinders: Mailing tubes can be cut into various lengths—four, five, six inches, etc.—to make a set of graduated cylinders. Be sure to cut evenly so that the cylinders won't fall over when the kids attempt to order them from smallest to largest.

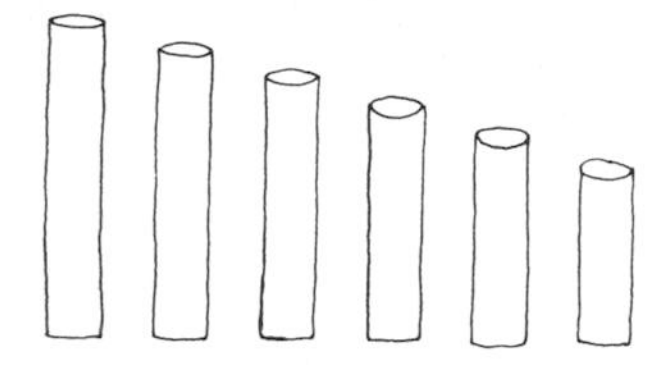

Sequence Cards: We use a set of cards with pictures representing a logical series of events to help kids develop their understanding of sequencing. For classroom use, we laminate the pictures with clear contact paper so that they are more durable. We might, for instance, have a set of three cards, like the ones pictured here. We'll ask the kids to put them in order; "Which picture 'goes' or 'happens' first?"

Memory Games: Kids also enjoy memory games. One of the old standbys is to have the first player say, "I'm going to Boston [or Disneyland or someplace the kids can relate to] and I'm going to take a ______." The next player repeats the sentence and the object the last player has named and adds a new object, and so on.

A similar type game is to have a collection of objects on a tray. The children look at the objects for a few seconds and try to fix them in their memories. Then they close their eyes, and you remove one object. When they open their eyes, they try to guess which object has been removed. Or you might make a "parade" of small objects, like the one pictured here. Let the child study it, then tell him to close his eyes while you rearrange the order. Then, let him try to put the parade back in the same order.

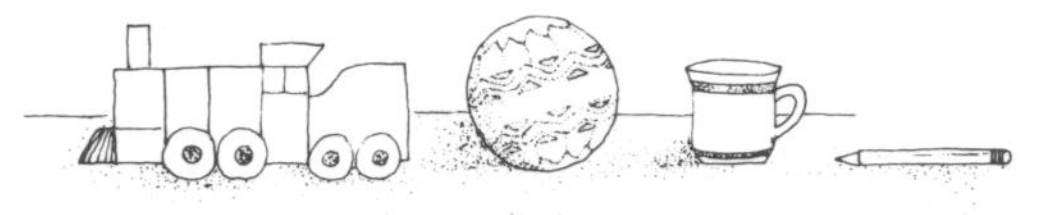

The kinds of readiness activities we've discussed in the last two chapters encompass a wide variety of skills and abilities. They are things most children develop quite naturally in the course of their play. Children who have environments rich in these kinds of play opportunities are well prepared for reading. Different children will develop these readiness skills at different rates. There can be no exact timetable. Generally, most children have developed these skills and are fairly proficient by the age of five or six, but other children will develop them earlier or later.

The next chapter describes the first steps in the Key Word method of teaching reading. One of the advantages of the Key Word method is that it can be used regardless of the child's level of readiness skills.

Parents who are working with their own children and providing lots of opportunities for developing oral language, perceptual skills, and other readiness skills can at the same time begin with the Key Word Cards, even if the child's readiness skills are not all that well developed. In fact, the Key Word Cards will help further develop many of these readiness skills. Teachers, who often have children with widely varying levels of readiness skills, will appreciate the fact that all their students can use the exact same reading materials.

Of course, the more "ready" a child is, the faster he will progress in learning to read. If a child has difficulty with the Key Word method, make sure that he has plenty of opportunities to develop the readiness skills that we have discussed at the same time as he is working on his Key Words.

4

THE NITTY GRITTY: KEY WORDS AND STORIES

On the last day of school each year, in the flurry of the final cleanup, we always turn up a set or two of them, stuffed here or there in the most unlikely places—a child's lost or abandoned Key Words, a set of tattered and worn index cards strung together on a shower curtain or notebook binder ring. On each, a word is printed. The first ones are written in our own practiced adult letters. Then, in the shaky, uncertain hand of the beginning writer, the string of words continues until, finally, the somewhat firmer, more sure-of-themselves cards emerge, printed carefully, even painstakingly, in the child's own evolving, personal style of handwriting. This individual style of handwriting will someday serve to identify the child as surely as his fingerprints.

Even though the style of handwriting may not yet be formed enough to unmistakably identify the author, the selection of words usually does. This set belongs to Peter: first a string of superheroes: *Batman, Superman*—the all-powerful fantasy heroes, creatures beyond the fears and problems of us mere mortals (rather typical choices in the early, somewhat scary first days of school). Then later come the home words: *Mommy, Daddy, Stewart* (brother), *Sissy* (sister). From his angry days, we

find *bomb, fight, explosion*; from his gentle days, *hug, friend*; from the days when he could allow it, the fearful ones, *monsters* and *ghost*, the nightmare words; and then, another string of superheroes, this time the cast of *Star Wars*.

Each set of cards is a record of the academic and personal journeys their authors have taken in our classroom that year.

The words that turn up on the children's Key Word Cards are rarely the ones listed on the State Department of Education's official grade-level vocabulary lists. Thank God! How frightening to have a child who asked for words like *look, see, as, many, because, if, off*. What would you say to such a child? No, the mad bomber—with his (or, more rarely, her) word cards full of explosions, kabooms, and fights, and later, the stories full of unbelievable violence in which he cheerfully reports his plans to level the school (with you in it)—is infinitely preferable.

The really good words are the ones that come from within, that are charged with meaning for the child. These Key Words are vivid, intense, alive words. They are a far cry from the emotionally sterile vocabularies of most beginning reading programs, for they are words that are part of the child's inner being: his heart, his feelings, his fears. Because they are already part of him, these Key Words are easily recognized and learned.

Of course, not all children's word cards are full of personal meaning, at least not at first. In the early days, when we first sit down with the child and explain that we are going to help them begin to learn to read and that we want them to pick a word they'd like to learn, it is not always an instant success. With some children, it takes a bit of time before we are admitted to their inner worlds and get their really meaningful words.

Step One: Getting the Key Word

With very young children, the fours and fives (or sometimes even threes), or with ones who have not yet developed sophisticated readiness skills, you may need to explain that words are written with certain kinds of marks called letters. Children are often confused about the difference between numbers and letters at this point, so if questioned, we explain that certain kinds of marks make words and other kinds make numbers, which are for counting or for telling "how many." (This is actually not the most accurate of explanations, but it seems to satisfy most children, at least for the time being). After we have told the children what we have in mind, we show them the white three by five-inch index cards that we use for the Key Words. We generally buy the kind with holes punched in the top corners for convenience since we store them on rings to prevent them from being lost.

The rings are the easiest, cheapest storage method that we've found, but almost any sort of container will do. Many of the parents we've worked with have used simple metal or wooden file card boxes (appropriately decorated by the child, of course). But they're too expensive for the classroom, and the cards on the rings are easy to flip through for a quick review.

After we show the cards and rings to the child, we say something like "Now we want you to give us a word that you would like to learn." If we put it this way, rather than asking, "Would you like to give me a word?," we get a better response. "Would you like to..." approaches can too easily set the scene for negative "don' wanna" responses. The child may feel threatened by having to answer a direct question. A clear statement of what you want is much easier for the child to deal with, and you're more likely to get a positive reaction. Some children will respond immediately; others will mull over the problem for quite a while. In the early stages, we try to allow the child a good bit of time to choose a word, but if the task seems too overwhelming or too confusing for the child, we'll help him along by telling him about a word that a child in another class in another year chose, or by asking about his favorite animal or food or TV show. If necessary, we'll give him a word, something to do with some special interest or preference of his.

It doesn't concern us if, in the first days, a child "copies" the word of another child or relies on us to supply the words. That's fine, whatever it takes to make that child feel comfortable. His own words will come.

Most of the parents we've known who have done Key Words with their children don't have too much of a problem getting words from their youngsters. The trust is already there. The parent knows the private, inner world of the child where the best and most easily learned of the Key Words originate. The more common problem for parents, and less often for teachers, is too many words. On the first day, the child wants not one, but two or three or five or ten or even more words. What to do when this happens? It depends on the child, on his level of readiness skills.

As we mentioned earlier, that's a part of the beauty of the Key Word approach to teaching. It can be used with any child, regardless of the level of readiness. Of course, the more "ready" a child is, the faster the learning will progress. A child whose visual discrimination abilities are immature simply will not be able to distinguish between very many different word cards and identify the visual patterns that make up his various words. But even such a child can begin, however slowly, to learn to read. In fact, the word card process will help to develop these skills.

Deciding where to cut off the avalanche of words that sometimes happens can be a bit tricky if the child is clamoring for more. But it is important not to give the child more than he can realistically handle. It can be very discouraging to a child to find that the precious words that meant so much on the first day are just a jumble of meaningless marks two days later because there are too many for any to be remembered clearly. Try to gauge a child's capabilities from what you know of his readiness skills. Unless he already knows the letters of the alphabet and how to read at least a few sight words, try to limit him to one word per day. Besides, it's always better to quit while the child's enthusiasm is high, before he gets tired. Thus, returning to the cards is an anticipated event.

Step Two: Writing on the Key Word Card

Once the word has been selected, we print it in the largest possible letters on the index card while the child watches. We generally use a wide-tip marker so that our letters are broad and thick and easily seen.

Parents are frequently concerned that their printing isn't standard or that the way they form their letters may vary too much from word to word. They worry that all of these imperfections will confuse their children. We try to reassure them by showing them cards we've written, which are hardly masterpieces of calligraphy, and by explaining that children develop the ability to easily recognize the general form of the letter despite variations in print or type style. Size is really more important, especially with young children, whose natural childhood farsightedness might make looking at smaller letters a strain. Of course, proper spelling is important. Don't be proud. Use a dictionary if you need one. We still have to look up *Brontosaurus* despite the fact that it is a frequently requested word among our five-year-old dinosaur buffs.

We also use both lower-case and upper-case letters on the word cards. If a word is a proper noun (the name of a particular place or person or thing), it should be capitalized. Here again, parents often worry that introducing both capital and lower-case letters at the same time will be too confusing. In our early years of teaching, we felt the same way, but over the years we've decided that teaching proper usage of the upper- and lower-case letters right from the start is best. We've found that it is often difficult to break the habit of using only upper-case or only lower-case letters when it comes time for children to write their own stories and books. It's much easier to teach both forms for a letter right at the beginning than to try to break a habit later.

As we slowly write the word that the child has given us, we sound out each individual letter. This is the child's first introduction to phonics, or the sounding out of words. For some children, this simple introduction is enough to provide them with a strong foundation in phonics. They catch on to it right away, and before you know it, they can sound out new words all by themselves. Most children, though, will need more work in phonics, which we provide through the games and activities described in the next chapter.

Once we've written the word and sounded out the letters, we repeat the word and then ask the child to say the word. Next, we go back over the word, pointing to each letter and saying something like "This is the letter '*bee*' and in your word it makes the *b* sound."

The exact sequence of the steps that follow will depend upon the particular child and his abilities. For the very youngest ones or the children who still need to develop fine muscle control, we go back over the word, explaining that we want the child to trace over the letters with his finger and sound out or say the letter names along with us. Sometimes we'll hold the child's hand and help guide it over the letters, or perhaps he'll do it without our guidance.

If we're working with children who've had plenty of cutting, painting, pasting, and scribbling experience and can control a pencil, we'll tell them that we want them to trace over the word with a pencil twice. As they write, we'll help them say first the name and then the letter sounds.

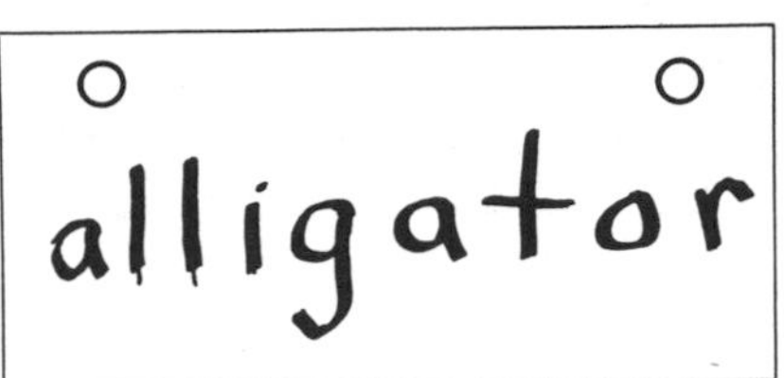

Here again, when we ask the child to trace over the word, we try to avoid saying "Can you trace over this word?" because if he can't, he might feel inadequate. If he's not sure, he simply won't reply or will say no. We try to avoid setting up a negative situation by simply saying, "Now I want you to do what I've just done; trace over the letters," as we place the card in front of the child. If he hesitates, we'll say something like "Here, let's do it together" and help him trace over the word.

The eventual goal is to get the child to the point where he can trace over the letters with a pencil by himself and repeat the letter names and sounds without prompting. Children who have difficulty tracing over the letters may need more of the fine muscle and eye-hand coordination exercises and activities described in chapter 3 as a supplement to their word cards. Children who don't already know the alphabet and the letter names and sounds will benefit from the games described in the beginning of the next chapter.

We sometimes cut sandpaper letters to paste on the word cards for children who have a great deal of perceptual difficulty. Such children may "see" things differently than the rest of us, and the additional tactile stimulation of the rough sandpaper will help reinforce the lessons they are trying to learn.

After the children have gotten to the point where they can trace over the letters with a pencil or crayon by themselves, the next step is copying the word right on the card underneath the letters we have printed.

In this copying step, we often find upper/lower-case mistakes. On the card pictured here, for instance, the child has copied the words *Star Trek* using an upper-case instead of a lower-case letter. It is important when correcting these mistakes that you spend at least twice as much time praising what's right as you do pointing out mistakes. We try to find a "lovely *s*" or a "fine *t*" that the child has made, or to praise the improvement in his handwriting. However, it is important to call a spade a spade. Your praise must be genuine or the child will feel that you are patronizing him.

Once you've given some praise, then you can gently correct the mistake, explaining why it's wrong. For instance, with the Star Trek card, we explained to the child that capital letters are often used at the beginning of words, but only very rarely in the middle of a word. Then we'll say something along the lines of "Now you need to fix that up." Once again, try to avoid asking questions like "Can you fix it?" The child may truthfully need to say no or attempt to avoid the task by saying "I can't."

Step Three: Reinforcing the First Words with Drawings in the Key Word Books

To help the children remember the Key Word, we get them to draw a picture of the word. This step is important, for it helps give the child more experience with the word which will help plant that word firmly in his memory.

The first drawings are done in the Key Word Books, which are simple affairs, just a few sheets of paper that the children have stapled together to form little booklets. Sometimes, if the classroom budget allows, we'll splurge on inexpensive little folders with metal paper fasteners to hold the pages together.

Some of the parents we've worked with have bought lovely blank books from art supply stores, intending to immortalize their children's first forays into literacy. Such books are usually bound so tightly that the pages won't lie flat enough to allow the child to write on them easily. Better, perhaps, to save the little booklets and bind them by one of the methods described at the last chapter.

After the word has been traced or copied, we give the child the Key Word Book and tell him that we want him to draw a picture to go with his word. We've found that kids enjoy it when we add a bit of variety to this procedure from time to time. Sometimes we'll put out our supply of old magazines, let the kids cut out pictures that illustrate their words, and paste them in their Key Word Books; other times they'll cut out letters of different colors, sizes, and shapes to spell out their Key Word. Peel off or "lick 'em" stickers are coveted treasures. The pictures on the stickers don't necessarily have anything to do with the Key Word, but pasting stickers around their drawings seems to delight kids. Once, we scrounged a box of small, clear plastic circles with black disks that jiggled around inside the circles, the kind of things that are used for eyes on comic greeting cards. We could have bought our way into the tastiest lunch boxes in the class that day. Children were literally begging each other to trade their assigned Key Word times for fear the treasures would run out before their turns came.

After the child has drawn, painted, pasted, or glued his picture, he'll usually bring it back so we all can admire it. We'll write the word on his drawing and, if time permits, repeat the

tracing and copying process. Generally, we try to avoid having the child draw pictures on the word card itself. If the drawing is on the word card, the child tends to focus on the picture as a clue to remembering, rather than on the letters of the word itself.

Sometimes a child will return to us with a drawing that has absolutely nothing at all to do with his Key Word. Generally, this happens in cases where the child has "copied" his word, has relied upon us for a word, or has hesitated, eyes roving around the room, and finally come up with some innocuous word like *window*. That's O.K., but sometimes the drawing can help us get at words closer to the child's inner world, words that will be remembered easily. For instance, one day a little girl, after much prodding, chose the word *table*. When she brought her word book back to show us her work, she had drawn a house on fire. "Hmm, that doesn't look like a table." Laughing at us, since she had already forgotten all about the "table," she said, "Oh, no, it's a fire, my house is burning down." So, we wrote "Fire! My house is burning down" on her picture, and the next day, that child's Key Word is, of course, fire.

Step Four: Reinforcing the Key Words with Stories in the Key Word Book

The next step is getting the child to tell us a story about the Key Word, which we write in his Key Word Book.

Like the drawings, the stories reinforce the Key Word and help the child to remember it. In addition, the stories familiarize kids with commonly used words that don't normally appear on word cards. Most of the words that the children choose for their word cards are nouns. Less exciting but frequently used words like *a, the, and, it, he, she, they, them* and *us* never appear on the word cards. Verbs, too, are rarely seen on word cards, especially simple ones like *saw, am, look,* and *was*. Yet, children need to learn to read these words. As they dictate story after story, and these words appear again and again, the children learn to recognize them.

The exact point at which the child makes the transition from drawings to stories depends on the individual child. Some children are ready for stories with their very first Key Words. If they are familiar with the alphabet, know how to form at least some of the letters, and have a story to tell, they may skip the drawing phase altogether.

The transition from drawing to story usually occurs quite naturally. A really good Key Word, one that is important to that child, almost always has an explanation or a story that goes with it. The case of the little girl who chose the word *table*, yet drew a picture of a burning house, is a good example. Once she had made a "fire" word card, she began to talk about the picture she had drawn. As she spoke, we wrote down what she was saying, and that became her first Key Word Story.

A fire came to my house. It fired all over. It fired all over my house. There was a noisy fire engine. I said, "Hi, Fireman."

Some children will be full of wonderful stories before they are actually ready to benefit from having them written down. If they are still working on controlling a pencil or learning the alphabet, there is usually not much of an advantage to writing out their story. They will not be able to recognize common sight words or even their own Key Words in the stories. Too many letters and too many words may only serve to confuse them at this point. However, there are no hard and fast rules. If a child asks for a story or has a particularly important one to tell, we may write that child's story even though, on a strictly academic level, they may not be able to understand the symbols.

When they are first making the transition from drawing to story, kids usually shift back and forth. One day they may do a story and the next day just a drawing. This is a natural part of the process. If a child has written a story before we felt that he was ready, we encourage the shift back to drawings; otherwise, we encourage the stories.

More rarely, we have children who we feel are ready for stories, yet the natural moment for the transition never seems to happen. In this case, we might show the child a word card and story that another child from a previous year's class has written. Often, this child will copy the other child's story or tell a version of a favorite story or fairy tale. This is fine. Eventually, that child will feel comfortable enough with the process to let his own stories come out.

Sometimes if they cannot think of a story, we'll just start talking about the word. For example, if a child chooses what we call "home words," names of the people and animals in his household, we might ask him what his mommy or daddy or brother did last night or to tell us who "Mumford" is. When we find out that Mumford is the family cat, then we get the story of how Mumford came into the household or a tale of one of Mumford's exploits. As the child starts to talk, we grab our pens and begin to write.

Sometimes children ramble on and on with their stories, which is fine, but not too practical in an overcrowded classroom. Parents may find that they can allow more time for longer stories. Still, at first, it is usually a good idea to stick to the three-, four-, or five-sentence stories; otherwise, the narrative can get pretty jumbled and incoherent.

If we have a limited time to work on these stories, we find that it is best to let the kids know beforehand that we only have five minutes. This way, the child doesn't get the feeling that we are cutting him off because his story is dumb or boring. Of course, we sometimes get stories that are too important to interrupt. For instance, one day a little girl chose the word *kiss* and then launched into a long, involved tale about how she had been playing in the front yard and a little boy who was apparently severely crippled with palsy came up to her and kissed her. She had a lot of confused feelings about this episode that she needed to work out, so, of course, we didn't interrupt this story. If time runs out on less intense stories, we may have to interrupt and make plans to continue the story next time.

While we are writing, the child sits right next to us so he can watch as we write. Most children tell their stories in long, run-on sentences strung together by "ands," "ors," and "thens." At this point, we don't separate their stories into sentences. Heaven help you if your authors start to suspect you are editing their work! And they will catch you at it, once they've gotten slick enough to recognize these common words. No, at this point, we don't concern ourselves with grammar. For too many children, such correction is like saying that their stories are wrong or unacceptable. So, if a child says, "There was this monster and he didn't like nobody," that's what we write.

Once we've gotten the story down, we read it aloud to the child. It often happens that when we reread the story, the child's grammatical errors will leap off the page at him and he'll ask us to correct the mistake. In this case, we do make the correction.

When you are writing the story, be sure to leave a good deal of space between the lines, for the next step involves underlining the Key Word and, later, copying it under the text.

Here again, the exact sequence of steps will vary from child to child. Some children need a good deal of help finding and underlining the Key Words in the story. They may need to practice tracing over the word in the story before they move to actually copying the word underneath. The goal here is to move the child to the point where he can find, underline, and copy the Key Word by himself. Eventually, he will be able to recopy and reread the story all by himself. At this point, he will be ready to move to the next stage of the Key Word process, writing his own stories. But we're getting ahead of ourselves. Perhaps a specific example of how the Key Word process works is in order.

This Key Word and Story belong to a five-year-old named Markie. One day Markie had been playing in the bushes outside the classroom, and in class she asked for the word *butterflies*. We wrote it on her card. Then she copied it all by herself.

"Tell me a story about your word, Markie," we asked.

"Well," she said, "Butterflies everywhere! And I catched one. And I put it back where it was. And I think it was happy."

Then we underlined the Key Word, *butterflies*, in her story. We traced over the word and, since Markie already knew the letter names, we only sounded the word out phonetically as we traced. Then we reread the story. Markie was so pleased with her story that she decided to illustrate it and to trace over all the words in her story. Then she ran to proudly show her work to her friends.

Once stories are written, they are usually passed around. The children read each other's work, with constant references made back to the author for help with words new to that reader.

The stories are kept in the Key Word Books, looseleaf notebooks or binders, and are the private property of each child. The children may choose whether or not they want to share their stories with others. In most cases, the children are eager to share their work, but occasionally, stories get written that children are not quite ready to share with a group, and this must be respected.

We never criticize the content of these stories, even if we learn that the young author is planning to bomb our homes, burn down the school, or "cut all the trees in the world down to the ground and wreck everything in the world." It is not unusual for children's stories to contain extreme violence, especially those stories that revolve around dreams they've had. Stories about brothers and sisters can be particularly murderous. Kids will often report their plans to do away with their siblings in most cheerful terms. Children's freedom to say what they're feeling is vital to the whole Key Word process. Unless children trust you to accept their inner worlds without censure, they won't let you in. If the Key Words don't come from that private world, they are just as meaningless as the preprogrammed, state-approved vocabulary lists. You might as well return to the apple-pie world of Dick and Jane.

The stories we get from children are so much richer and more real than the stories in adult-written reading books. Unlike the respectable, happy reading books that ignore, hide, suppress, and distill the drama out of life, the children's stories are full of passion, conflict, and emotion.

The stories our children write are so much more exciting. We reach into the children's minds and out comes all sorts of stuff, from declarations of love:

to expressions of fear:

stories about death:

The pony is asleep. It is flying up in the air. It will never wake up.

and unbelievable cataclysms:

Sometimes tales of great adventure:

I had a lot of fires not close to my house the last time Joey was there. He saw a fire starting. And

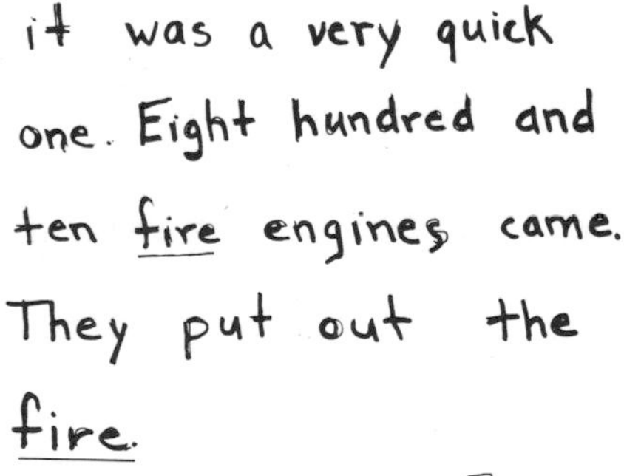

Sometimes tales of woe:

or anger:

Hilary is not my ~~Hilary~~ best friend no more.

And she can't come to my birthday party. She took my ball and said "na, na, na!"

And, of course, jealousy:

I hate my brother.
I hate my brother.
He gets to do everything.
he gets to do everything.
I don't get to do nothing.
I don't get to do nothing.
He makes messes. They think he's cute.
He makes messes. They think he's cute.

At times, though not at first, funny stories:

My toe moved...
Except I didn't move it. So I went in the bedroom and took off my shoe. A big bug crawled out! Auugh!

And sometimes a touch of whimsy:

and even a bit of poetry:

Ballet is wonderful.
Ballet is wonderful.

Ballet is nice.
Ballet is nice.

Ballet is easier than
Ballet is easier than

suckin' ice.
suckin' ice.

Oh, I've had some
Oh, I've had some
wonderful moments
Wonderful Moments
in my life.
in my life.

Of course, not all the stories we get are so easy to understand. Often, the stories, especially the first ones, are not completely logical or coherent, at least not what we adults consider logical and coherent. Take, for instance, this story, which was the first one written by a little boy who was to become the all-school expert on dinosaurs a few months later.

Dinosaurs eating ducks? Besides not being too logical, the story seems a little abrupt and full of rather large gaps. Still, we dutifully wrote what he dictated without comment, for we know that developing the art of telling a story takes some time. In a few short weeks, the logic of the narrative of this boy's story had improved considerably until he was dictating stories like this one:

> It was 150 million years ago.
> Dimetrodon saw a Stegosaurus.
> They fought. Dimetrodon was dead.
> Stegosaurus saw a Tyrannosaurus
> Rex. The Tyrannosaurus Rex
> went away. Then a Diplodocus
> came. Then another dinosaur
> named Brachiosaurus came. And
> they came to a pond
> that had no water. And all the
> dinosaurs died out. And a man digged
> and he saw a dinosaur bone. And
> that's how he knew there were
> dinosaurs. The End.

Sometimes children will begin to wander in the middle of their stories, obviously floundering, in which case a simple question from you can sometimes put them back on the track.

Once there was a big and medium and little pumpkins. And they had big and long legs. And they had arms. And they had eyes and teeth and a nose and two eyes. And two pairs of feet and two pairs of bodies.

And what happened to the big pumpkin? They were on a boat and the large pumpkin jumped in the water and a shark ate him.

We pulled the child back onto the track, giving her story some direction by asking her "What happened to the big pumpkin?" She repeated the question in her story and answered, perhaps not in the most logical or expected of ways, but it did direct her attention back to creating a story line. Through the injection of questions such as "What happened to. . .?" or "What happened next?" we begin to help the children shape their ability to create a logical composition that can be understood and shared by others.

What's more important than the effectiveness and creativity of the Key Word and Story activities is the emotional freedom they allow children. When children are encouraged to express their innermost feelings, they become healthier and happier. Take, for instance, a child who comes to school after having heard his parents have a huge blowup the night before. Well, if that child reads the story of another child about the horrible fight the other child's parents had, then his parents' fight becomes less frightening. After all, other people do it too. It's not so horrible that it can't be talked about (we all know that if something is too terrible to talk about, then it's *really terrible*).

The Key Word method can be especially effective when parents use it with their own children. It can help to build a stronger, firmer, more loving relationship, for it enables parents to participate intimately in the child's inner world. Moreover, it can open channels of communication between parent and child.

For example, this book was done by a youngster who was very mad at her mother that day.

From the cover it looks as if it might be one of those sweet little I-love-you notes that our children so often produce. The first page is a smiling mom—"My Mom?" Then the snafu—"My

Mom!" and a picture of a snarly, witchy-looking woman. The next illustration shows the wicked mother chasing the poor child around the house, spitting at her. (In order to protect the innocent, let us assure the readers that the mother in question has never chased her child around the house, much less spit on her.) The child continues to hide from this mean old mother. Finally, though, the child is caught and tossed in the back seat of the car (note the flailing arms and legs in the back seat) and taken to her wonderful father's house. And as the final clincher—a good-bye for meany mom from behind a closed door.

Obviously, there are a lot of things going on here. Some legitimate complaints, some deep confusions, and a bit of emotional bribery. As a result of making and reading this book, though, the mother and child involved came to talk about and deal with some important issues. It brought things to the surface that might otherwise have been glossed over or ignored, hidden, and repressed.

Often, children tell stories about themselves and their feelings, yet do not recognize that they are talking about themselves. For instance, one little girl told a story about a child who sold her little brother to the trash man, threw him in the garbage, and had him hauled off to the dump (a rather neat solution to the sibling rivalry problem). When asked who the little girl in the story might be, this child had absolutely no inkling that she was talking about herself. Or how about this one:

The child who wrote this story didn't realize, at least not on a conscious level, that he was talking about his own loneliness. A sensitive teacher or parent can use stories like this to help kids get in touch with their feelings.

Another interesting example of how children's emotional dilemmas are reflected in their work is the story below, which was written by another child who was suffering the pangs of sibling rivalry but had been told by the adults in her home that it was *not* O.K. to hate your brother once in a while and that it was quite naughty and wrong to say anything along those lines.

With the inevitable candor of a child the young author short-circuits her own sugary sweet "I love my brother," coming closer to her real feelings in the last line.

Parents and teachers who work with children writing their Key Stories are sometimes privy to the deepest anger and sadness of the children. The stories are often quite poignant and touching.

Whether the stories are funny or sad or angry or silly, they are charged with meaning and emotional content. This is what makes the process so exciting and what instills a love of and respect for language in the children.

Step Five: Reviewing the Key Words

After the children have chosen their first words and done their first drawings or stories, the review process begins. For the first few days, we review all their words each time. Later on, spot checks are enough to keep the words fresh in their minds. Children also review their words or, more accurately, "show them off" to each other. This helps them to remember their words and to learn new words from each other.

We have found that words that a child has "copied," that we have supplied, or that don't have real significance for the child are often not remembered. In such cases, we usually toss them, but not without consulting the child. If we come across such a word, we might say, "You know, I don't think this is really a special word for you. Maybe it doesn't belong on your ring, which is for your very own, most important words. What do you think?" Some children insist on keeping the word anyhow. For them, throwing a word out is like asking them to throw away an arm or a leg, so it's important to ask first.

This is another instance where you want to avoid those yes/no-type questions. Too many times if you say, "Do you want to keep it?" the child will automatically nod his head yes, whether he wants the card or not.

From time to time, all children forget or stumble over their words. This is quite natural. When this happens, referring back to the story or drawing, giving a clue to the child, will usually help him remember the word.

Children with very immature visual perception or perception problems, or who simply haven't learned the alphabet yet, may have trouble recognizing their Key Words. We make sure that these children have plenty of the kinds of opportunities described in chapter 3 and lots of time to play the games and activities described in the first part of the next chapter. But we don't stop the Key Word process.

One approach that worked well with a little girl who was having trouble remembering her Key Words was to reverse the roles of teacher and student. In fact, she invented this approach herself. One day, she took her Key Word ring and held up the first card, which said "monster." "What's this word?" she demanded in a strict and belligerent tone (which we winced to think she might have heard from us).

"Well, now, I'm not quite sure," we replied. "Let's see, that's a letter *m* there at the beginning of the word. Mmmmm. Milkshake? Marmalade? Mud pie?"

Laughing, she shook her head no at our foolishness.

"Well, let's see, after the *m*, there's an *o* and then an *n*, so that must be *mon*. . . ." By this time, she had remembered the word and generously stepped in and told us the word was *monster*, adding that we were doing very well. We would continue on like this, through her word cards, guessing the words we felt sure she knew instantly and spending more time on the ones we knew she was having difficulty with. She became, by the way, an excellent teacher, always full of praise for our successes.

We didn't explain this peculiarity to recommend it to you as a method of reviewing. In fact, it might be totally confusing to anyone who had not made up the rules himself. However, it illustrates a problem that often comes up with children who have trouble remembering their word cards. They may feel as if they are being tested and failing. It's important that the child experience success. Sometimes, it helps to review one or two drawings, talk about the words, and trace over them just before reviewing those same words. We have absolutely no qualms about "rigging" the review in this way. These children will eventually learn to recognize their Key Words. There is nothing to be gained by making them feel a sense of failure just because learning is not instantaneous and easy for them.

Another trick we use, especially with children whose powers of discrimination are poor, is to outline the shape of the Key Word with a bright red marker. This will help them to recognize the generalized form or pattern of the word, which is somewhat easier than recognizing the more complex pattern of the individual letters. Cutting the letters of their words out of sandpaper and pasting the letters on their cards will also help. When they trace over the sandpaper with their fingers, the tactile stimulation helps reinforce the form of the word. Or, if they have a fair amount of motor control, we'll give them a bottle of white glue. They trace over their Key Word with a line of glue and then pour sand or glitter over the card. After the glue or glitter has dried, they shake off the excess and the effect is the same as that of the sandpaper. Here again, we emphasize work on visual perception and alphabet games with these children in addition to their work with the word cards.

In addition to having spot reviews of the Key Words, we generally reread the stories in the Key Word books from time to time. This helps kids to learn frequently repeated words like *us, me, him, her, their, those, they, was, saw, and, because*, and so on.

If the child agrees, we'll read the story to the whole class. Parents can do the same at home, using the family as an audience. Eventually, the children will be able to read the stories themselves, at which point they will be ready to make the transition to journal writing, which is described in Chapter 6.

We generally work on Key Words, reviewing and adding new

words, at least three times a week. Our classrooms are organized in what is referred to as "open-style education." It would take another whole book to describe how to develop, organize, and run an open-style classroom. There are a number of such books. The ones we found most helpful are listed in the bibliography in the Appendix.

The fact that our classrooms are full of learning centers and games and activities that one, two, or more children can do independently allows us enough free time to work individually with each child in our class at least three times a week, even during the most hectic weeks. We get everyone started on independent activities and draw the children away one or two at a time for Key Word work. While one child is doing his drawing or copying his story, we'll draw another aside and begin work with him. The children know that this Key Word time is special and private and that interruptions are to be avoided as much as possible.

For parents working at home with their children, it's usually less of a problem to find time for Key Words. It only takes a few minutes each day. In fact, it needn't be every day. As one parent we were working with explained, "I don't have a regular everyday schedule. I just don't work that way, it's not my style or my daughter's. It's hard for me to imagine any kid who always wants to play the game at the same time every day, but I suppose some people are more regular about things. I'm considerably more casual, some would say haphazard, about it. The cards disappear for a week or two and then find their way back into our lives. One time we sort of stopped for a while and they turned up again a few weeks later when my daughter had taken her cat card and added an "apackopee s" [apostrophe s, something she'd learned on "*Electric Company*" or "*Sesame Street*"] and put the card in the cat's bed. That sort of started us up again."

Whether you and your child are as casual as this mother and daughter or more disciplined, as we are in the classroom, we think your children will benefit from the Key Word method. As teachers, we are always delighted with children who come to school having learned at least something about reading at home. It makes our job and the children's job that much easier.

Having children choose their own vocabularies, dictate, and later write their own stories has proven to be an effective teaching method. Kids are always interested in reading about themselves, and the activity combines reading and writing, composition and spelling, and increases vocabularies. And it's so much more interesting than traditional teaching. Recently, we visited an unfortunately typical classroom. Thirty children were bunched up in rows of desks, strenuously gripping pencils and dutifully copying the composition the teacher had written on the board, which went like this: "Today we had cooking class. We made Indian fry bread. It was delicious! We had fun!" Then we wandered into the next classroom and found thirty more kids copying a composition off the board: "Today we had cooking class. We made Indian fry bread. It was delicious! We had fun!"

Now, out of those sixty kids who made fry bread that day, there had to be at least one who thought it tasted terrible or who didn't have fun. So at least one kid, and probably a whole lot more, was being taught to lie and that language is just a polite convention, meaningless chatter that has nothing to do with the truth of thoughts and feelings. How unfortunate, when it would be so much more exciting, effective, and fun for both kids and teachers to learn reading and writing in other, more honest ways.

5

FUN AND GAMES: READING ACTIVITIES AND EXERCISES

We've had some kids who've started out with Key Words, whizzed through the writing of story after story and the next time we turned around, they were over in the corner reading the encyclopedia. (Well, perhaps that's a slight exaggeration.) At any rate, such kids are the exception rather than the rule. Most kids need more practice with phonic skills and with common sight words that don't conform to phonic rules and that aren't normally chosen as Key Words. For these children, we have concocted, created, and collected the games, activities, and exercises described in this chapter.

We use this game approach to learning because it's a lot more fun than drill and memorization. We've yet to meet a child who would not rather play a game of cards than sit at his desk and copy a word ten times in order to memorize it. It's a lot more entertaining to play bingo than to memorize a list of vocabulary words. And we've found that this game approach is more effective. Playing Concentration with a deck of sight-word cards will help kids learn those words much faster than any other teaching approach we've ever tried. It's a simple fact that kids learn better when they're enjoying themselves.

Incidentally, all of these games have passed the 100,000-mile test drive in our classes. No matter how "cutesy" we thought they were, we've eliminated the ones that sat on the shelves gathering dust or that were declared "dumb" or "boring" by our test drivers.

The games in this chapter are divided into two categories: those that teach phonic or "sounding out" skills and those that teach kids to recognize common sight words or help to build basic vocabularies. We use all of these games in our classrooms. Parents, because they don't need to meet the learning needs of a whole group of children, can pick and choose according to what skills their child needs help with and what looks like fun.

We generally rotate games in our classrooms throughout the school year. Parents may find that the same thing works well for them. If a game is getting a bit too familiar, is ignored, or starts gathering dust, we remove it for a couple of months. Then, when we bring it back, it seems fresh and new. Nor do we unload our whole closetful of goodies all at once. We introduce new games one at a time. This way, interest stays high and children aren't overwhelmed by too much all at once.

Many of the games in this chapter are made from shirt cardboard, tagboard (also called poster board), and index cards. Parents should find that these will hold up very well for use with their children, but the classroom teacher, especially if the games are to be used year after year, may find these materials a bit flimsy. Thus, teachers may want to glue playing boards made from shirt cardboards or tagboard to a sturdier piece of cardboard. Using Tri-wall cardboard, which consists of three layers of single-wall cardboard laminated together, will make your games virtually indestructible. Tri-wall is almost as sturdy as plywood.

You can make your own version of Tri-wall by gluing sheets of single-wall (the kind of cardboard used for most cartons) together with rubber cement. Apply the rubber cement to both surfaces and let it dry until it is tacky. Lay one sheet on top of the other so the corrugation is at cross-grain. Weigh the sheets down

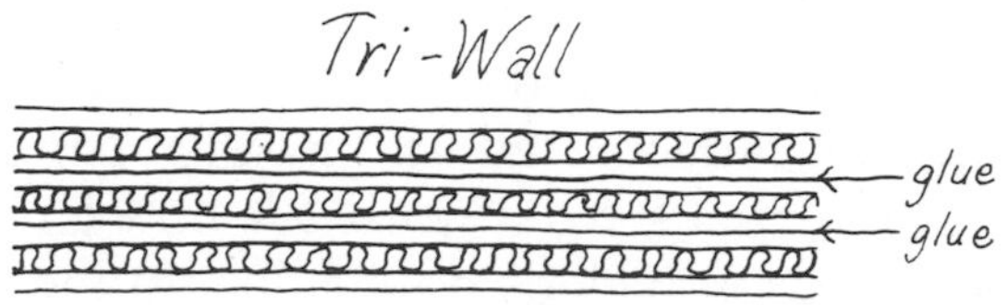

with a board or piles of books until dry. Tri-wall, which is a brand name, can be purchased fairly inexpensively. Look under "Boxes—Corrugated & Fibre" in the Yellow Pages. Call some of the companies listed and ask if they sell Tri-wall or if they can direct you to the Tri-wall distributor in your area. Tri-wall can also be ordered from the Workshop for Learning Things, a group of teachers, artists, and designers who have created a myriad of wonderful learning tools and ideas. Write to them at 5 Bridge Street, Watertown, MA 02172 for price and ordering information.

We also use blank index cards in a number of these games. Here again, parents will find that these are sturdy enough to hold up quite well until their children have mastered the skills that the particular game teaches. Teachers might want to invest a little extra time and energy in order to increase the life span of these games. Where appropriate, the index cards can be glued to a tagbord or cardboard backing or the cards can be cut from sturdier materials to begin with. Poster board often comes with a white side and colored side. The bright colors will make the cards more attractive and the thickness of the board will make them more durable.

For classroom use, we always "laminate" our game pieces with sheets of clear contact paper. That way, the games can be wiped clean whenever the coating of peanut butter and jelly gets too thick. We've found that index cards backed with colored contact paper and faced with clear contact paper make good cards for games that use decks of playing cards. They are sturdy, yet flexible enough to be shuffled.

It is important to make the games as attractive as possible, so that the kids will want to use them. Of course, what's attractive to you as an adult may be very different from what's attractive to a child. For instance, at the beginning of one school year, we made a game called a Feely Box, which we spray-painted white and wasted a number of hours decorating with an intricate flower border. Before the first month of school was over, our charming creation had been redecorated with a wallpaper covering of *Star Wars* comic book pages. So it goes. We now limit ourselves to a basic paint job and let the kids do the decorating. Sometimes our expertise at, say, drawing flowers is called into use, but always according to the children's plans.

Get the kids involved in making the games whenever

possible. Making the game, selecting the appropriate pictures, tracing letter stencils on cards, and so on, can be as educational as the game itself. The painting, coloring, cutting, and pasting will help them develop the eye-hand and fine muscle coordination they will need for writing. Besides, kids enjoy playing with games that they have helped make and are apt to take much better care of them.

You'll want to begin saving assorted sizes of boxes in which to store the games. The boxes should also be decorated and clearly labeled. We've found it helpful to label the storage boxes and game boards and to specify the place they are to be stored (drawer, shelf, or whatever) with some system—pictures or colored labels, for example. This makes it easier to teach the kids to clean up after themselves, and the games and all their little pieces stay intact.

Many of the games can be used in several different ways. We have tried to suggest alternative uses. You and your children will probably be able to invent even more uses. Some of the games and activities can be done independently by one child. Others can be done by two or more children on their own. Many of the activities are self-correcting so the children can check their own work. Almost all the games can be played by a parent and child together. If the game requires a group, parents can always invite some other children over to play.

The kids in our classes and the parents and children we've worked with have found the games and activities in this chapter enjoyable and effective as learning tools. We hope you will, too.

The Alphabet

We first introduce the letter names, sounds, and forms to the children in our work with the Key Words. At the same time, we use the games and activities described in this section to help familiarize kids with the alphabet.

Since we use both upper- and lower-case letters on the word cards, these alphabet games are also made with upper- and lower-case letters. You can avoid a lot of confusion when teaching the alphabet by referring to upper-case letters as "upper-case" or "capitals" and lower-case letters as "lower-case." It's the kind of letter you're talking about, not the size. If you use the terms "big" and "small," a child might think that b is a "big" letter and B is a "small" letter.

Of course, what's really important in learning to read is the sound the letter makes,* so be sure to emphasize the sound as well as the name when playing these games. We usually begin by teaching one sound per letter. These are the initial sounds we use in beginning phonics:

a as in *apple*
b as in *boy*
c as in *cat*
d as in *day*
e as in *egg*
f as in *frog*
g as in *go*
h as in *hat*
i as in *ink*
j as in *jump*
k as in *kettle*
l as in *lamp*
m as in mom
n as in *no*
o as in *ox*
p as in *pie*
q as in *queen*
r as in *run*
s as in *sit*
t as in *tap*
u as in *umbrella*
v as in *violin*
w as in *wash*
x as in *xylophone*
y as in *yellow*
z as in *zebra*

Two letters can cause a bit of confusion, *c* and *g*. Both these letters have two sounds, one "hard" and one "soft." For instance, the letter *c* may make the soft sound as in *city* or *circle* or, more frequently in beginning reading, the hard sound as in *cat* or *cake*. Likewise, *g* may be soft as in *giant* or *giraffe*, or it may be hard as in *go*, *green*, or *get*. We have a couple of specific activities to help familiarize kids with these hard and soft sounds.

Phonics, as you will see, is a rather inexact system. Many times a single letter will make several different sounds. The letter *x*, for instance, can make six separate sounds. The letters *ch* in combination can make the sound in the word *church*, the *k* sound in *choir*, and the *sh* sound in *chef*. Sometimes, the same sound can be made by many different letters. For instance, *ir*, *ur*, *er* can all make the same sounds as in *fir*, *burn*, and *her*. (In this case, the variations cause more problems in spelling than in reading.) It is important, then, that you communicate to kids that this phonic system is only a rough guideline, not a system of infallible laws.

*Technically speaking, letters don't "make" sounds, they represent them, but we use the word "make" in the beginning because it's easier for kids to understand what we mean.

Jumbo Alphabet

Materials:

52 3½ by 3½-inch squares of
  Tri-wall or triple-thick
  cardboard
Alphabet Patterns
  (see Appendix)
marking pens
mat knife
sandpaper (optional)

Construction:

Cut out the Alphabet Patterns in the back of this book. Paste one in the center of each of the cardboard squares. Use an Exacto knife or similar cutting tool to cut the letter out of the cardboard square. The square can then be used as a frame for the letter. It's a good idea to cover each of these letters with sandpaper so that the tactile sensation of the sandpaper will reinforce the information the children are trying to learn. Thus, their sense of touch as well as their eyes are helping to plant the shape of the letter forms in their minds. To make the set more attractive, you can paint the letters and squares or cover them with contact paper.

This alphabet can be used in many different ways. You might remove the letters from their squares and let the child replace them in the proper squares. To start this simple puzzle activity, give the child two or three letters and frames; then, after he has some success with that, add more letters and frames.

The frames or the letters themselves can be used as stencils for forming letters. The child simply traces around the letter or inside the frame and then colors or paints the letter he has traced.

After the child can fit all the letters into the frames, sit down and review the letter names and the sounds that the letters make. Then help the child put the letters in their proper sequence. Here again, make it easy at first, using only three or four letters. Once the child knows those names and sounds and can put them in correct order, add two or three more letters until he has mastered the alphabet.

A group of two or more kids can use a timer and try to beat the clock as they fit the puzzle pieces and put the letters in alphabetical sequence. This works well if a parent and child or older and younger child play it together. The game is exciting and the younger child will learn from the older one or the parent as the game is played.

Another task that we sometimes assign a child or group of children is to match the upper-case and lower-case letters. Here again, it's best to start with just a few letters. Choose the most obvious matches, letters that are very similar in both upper and lower case. After the easier ones (*c, k, o, s, u, v, w, x, z*) have been mastered, add more difficult ones until the child can match all the upper- and lower-case letters correctly. To make this game self-correcting, you can write the matching lower-case letter on the back of the upper-case frame and vice versa. By turning over the frames, the children can check their own or each other's work.

One game that our kids enjoy playing with the Jumbo Alphabet is to hide a letter somewhere and have the others hunt for it. When someone finds the hidden letter, make a point of saying the letter name and the sound it represents. This game can be played with one child or with a large group. It is particularly good with kids of various age levels, for the younger ones will learn from the older ones. To enhance this game with more sophisticated kids, ask them to guess what letter has been hidden by riffling through all of the unused letters and determining what's missing.

The possibilities are endless. You and your children should be able to dream up lots of games using the Jumbo Alphabet. One clever kid in one of our classes organized a sort of obstacle course on the playground, putting an *A* on the jungle gym, a *B* on the crawl-through tunnel, a *C* on the swing, a *D* on the sandbox, and everyone had to crawl, climb, and swing their way through the alphabet. Invent some of your own games and activities and remember to stress both the letter names and sounds when you are playing.

Alphabet Match-ups

Materials:
52 pieces of cardboard
approximately 3 by 5 inches
52 pictures, cut from
magazines, that repre-
sent the letters of the
alphabet
scissors
felt-tip markers

Construction:

On the right half of each card, paste the picture you have selected, and on the left half, write an upper- or lower-case letter of the alphabet. If you want to make the game more durable, cover the cards with clear contact paper. Then, following a zigzag or squiggly line, cut the card in half. Commercial versions of this game are available, but they have one drawback: The pieces are cut so that only the correct picture and letter will fit together, and that's the snag. The kid doesn't have to pay attention to the letters to finish the activity; he only has to have some rudimentary puzzle skills. Our improved version is much the same, only we cut some of the cards in exactly the same way so that some of the pieces are identical. Thus, the child really has to match the letter with the pictured object that starts with the sound. We make identical pieces for commonly confused letters like *b/d, m/n,* and *j/g.* On the back of each correctly matched pair, we draw a colored line so that the child can check his own work by turning the fitted pieces over and making sure the colored lines match.

You can also make an upper-case, lower-case match-up set. Instead of using a picture and letters on your card, write the upper-case and corresponding lower-case letter. Here again, cut identical pieces for some of the easily confused letters and mark the backs with colored lines for self-correction.

When you've finished, give the sets of cards to the child and let him attempt to match them up correctly. Remember to start with a few easy ones, and once he's had some success, add some other match-ups.

Printing Block Letters

Materials:

52 small wooden blocks (available at school supply stores)
velvet-covered contact paper
indelible marking pen
mat knife
stamp pad or damp sponge soaked in a solution of two parts poster paint and one part white glue

Construction:

First you will need to draw the letters of the alphabet on your contact paper. The letters should be drawn small enough to fit on one face of the wooden blocks. *A, H. I,* etc. are reversible and won't cause any problem, but since these contact paper letters will become the printing surface, you will have to draw most of the letters backwards. Then using the mat knife, cut the upper- and lower-case letters of the alphabet from the contact paper. Stick a letter on one face of the block. Write the same letter on the opposite face of the block.

Children enjoy using these blocks to print signs, labels, word cards, or name tags or to make graphic designs. You might ask a child to print the alphabet with the blocks. Or, if the child is having trouble with his word cards, he might print them on a page that could be added to his Key Word Book. For children who are having trouble with reversals and find it difficult to distinguish letters like *b* and *d*, printing pages of *b*'s and *d*'s decorated with pictures or drawings of words can be a helpful exercise.

Alphabet Books

Materials:
unlined paper
construction paper
old magazines
scissors
glue
a stapler or a hole puncher
  and yarn
crayons, paints, or felt-tip
  markers

Construction:

The kids can make these themselves. First they make a booklet by stapling the unlined paper together between two sheets of construction paper or by punching holes in the paper and tying the booklet together with yarn.

The kids can turn these blank booklets into Alphabet Books in a number of different ways. They might, for example, use their printing blocks to print an upper- and lower-case letter on each page. Then they can draw or paint pictures of objects whose names begin with that letter on the page. They might trace the letters onto the page using the Jumbo Alphabet, or simply write the letter themselves and cut pictures from magazines to decorate the pages. Another variation is to give them a stack of magazines and let them choose a letter and cut out as many different forms of the letter as they can find. Then they make a collage on one page of their book. Sometimes, we might ask them to choose a letter and make it into a picture of something that begins with that letter. Ask them to make the whole alphabet this way.

Compact Alphabet

Materials:

26 empty makeup compacts with mirrors
tagboard
rubber cement
old magazines
scissors
felt-tip marker

Construction:

Clean any leftover makeup out of the compact. Cut pieces of tagboard to fit the empty makeup compartments and glue them in place. Cut pictures that represent the letters of the alphabet (a pumpkin for *Pp*, a ball for *Bb*, etc.) and glue them to the tagboard. In one corner of the picture, write the letter it represents. You can also substitute letters for pictures once kids become more familiar with the alphabet.

The kids enjoy opening these compacts and watching their lips as they pronounce the words. This exercise is particularly good for children who have difficulties pronouncing or hearing certain letters. We might sit down with such a child and open, for instance, the *Bb* and *Dd* compacts, helping that child to note the difference in how his lips move. This game can also be used to help children learn the consonant blends and digraphs explained on pages 124–126.

Alphabet Feely Box

Materials:
cardboard carton
tape
mat knife
Jumbo Alphabet letters

Construction:

To make the Feely Box, we seal the top and bottom of a cardboard carton with tape and cut two holes in one end so the kids can stick their hands inside.

Slip some of the letters from the Jumbo Alphabet inside the box (not too many at first). Ask the child to find a certain letter by reaching into the box. Since the kids can't see the letters, they have to rely on their sense of touch. For beginners, we often write the letter on a piece of paper and lay it on top of the box to aid them in their search.

We might ask the children to find the letter, asking for the letter by name, or we might say, "Find the letter that your name starts with" or "Find the letter that makes the 'mmmmmm' sound."

Children can work on this without a grownup's help if you give them a series of pictures of various objects and ask them to match the pictures with the letters in the Feely Box. As they find each letter, they lay it on top of the picture. The game can be made self-correcting by printing the correct upper- and lower-case letter on the back of the picture.

Just to keep things interesting, we sometimes slip a dish of Slime (a delightfully yucky substance, sold in most toy stores, which seems to fascinate young kids), cooked noodles, or peeled grapes into the Feely Box. The joke is enjoyed by everyone, but don't be surprised if you find a dish of Slime slipped into your lunch box one day. Turn about is fair play!

Alphabet Rubbings

Materials:
paper
crayons, pastels, or charcoal
sticks

Construction:

Lay your paper on raised letters found on buildings, gravestones, manhole covers, or wherever. Rub your crayons, pastel, or charcoal stick across the paper until the word appears.

The excitement of getting out of the classroom or house and the adventure of finding words and letters makes this activity a real favorite with kids. It is particularly useful for kids who are having difficulties learning the letter forms. Younger ones can collect a whole alphabet; older ones, a whole new vocabulary of "found" words.

Upper/Lower-Case Chant

Materials:
a chalkboard and chalk or a
large sheet of paper and a
marking pen

Construction:

Select one letter and print a line of lower- and upper-case letters across your chalkboard or sheet of paper.

This game is usually more fun with a group, although with the proper enthusiasm, it could work with an individual child and adult. We ask the kids to "read" the line of letters as we point to them, using a big, deep voice for the capitals and a small, squeaky, mouselike voice for the lower-case letters. The game can be varied by using more than one letter or by including more than one row of letters. This game not only helps the kids learn the difference between upper- and lower-case letters, but gives them practice in reading a line of print from left to right and in moving from the end of one line to the beginning of another.

Lower- and Upper-Case Match-ups

Materials:
3 12-egg cartons
one 30-egg flat
78 small, round self-adhesive labels (available at stationery stores)
marking pen
scissors

Construction:

Print the lower-case letters from *a* to *z* on one set of labels and stick them on the "bumps" of the large egg flat. Next cut twenty-six "cup" sections out of the small egg cartons. Make another set of lower-case letter labels and stick them inside each cup. Then print the alphabet in upper case on the last set of labels and stick them on the outside of each cup.

The child is given the egg flat and the egg cups and asked to match the upper- and lower-case letters by placing the cup over the correct "bump" on the flat. Since the correct lower-case letter is printed on the inside of each cup, the game is self-correcting.

Hard/Soft Books

Materials:
unlined paper
construction paper
paste
old magazines
scissors
a stapler or a hole puncher and yarn
crayons, paints, or felt-tip pens

Construction:

The kids can make these themselves by stapling the unlined paper between construction-paper covers or by punching holes in the paper and tying the booklets together with yarn.

Explain to the children that the letters c and g each have two sounds, one that we call hard and one that we call soft. Give them some examples of words that have the hard sound and ones that have the soft sound. Ask them to make two books, one with hard and one with soft sounds, by drawing pictures in their books or by looking through magazines and cutting out pictures.

Hard and Soft G/C Sort

Materials:

- 2 sheets of shirt cardboard or tagboard of the same approximate size
- blank index cards
- pictures cut from old magazines
- scissors
- paste

Construction:

Divide your sheets of cardboard in half. Write the capital and lower-case *Gg* on each half of one and a capital and lower-case *Cc* on each half of the other. To clarify the hard/soft difference, write and illustrate a word that begins with a hard sound on one half of the board and a word that represents a soft sound on the other half. Then make a set of cards with pictures representing hard and soft words that begin with these letters.

Use this game to help children who are having trouble learning the hard and soft sounds. Ask them to sort the cards according to whether they have the hard sound, like the picture and word on one side of the board, or the soft sound, like the picture and word on the other half of the board.

Body Letters

In this game, the kids make the letters themselves, using their own bodies. As a group game, this works well when the kids are feeling restless or with active kids who seem to learn best when their bodies are in motion. Two or more kids pair off and the leader assigns them a letter. Then the kids use their bodies either lying on the floor or standing up, to form the letters. It's a giggly, roly-poly exercise and the kids really have to think about the letter forms in order to "pantomime" the letter. Later on, teams can choose simple sight words from a hat and spell them out for the rest of the group to guess.

Guess the Letter

Kids always enjoy guessing games. You might try tracing letters in the air with your fingers and have them take turns guessing the invisible letters. Our children love having letters traced on their backs and trying to guess the letter. This game usually ends up with a lot of rolling, cuddling, hugging, or tickling, which is just fine.

Oral Games

These simple games will help kids learn the letter sounds. The simplest game of all is to pick a letter and ask the kids to say as many words as they can that begin with that sound. Say, for example, that you use the letter *m*. Give a couple of words that start with *m* like *Mary*, *marble*, and *mama*. Then get the kids to join in.

We are always surprised at how well very young kids can play this game. Apparently, even if they cannot recognize the letter visually, their ears can recognize the sound. Parents can play this game with their children at odd times—in the car, in the tub. It doesn't have to be a formal lesson for kids to learn. Sometimes when we play this game with a group of kids, the ones who can write will keep lists of words. If possible, have a letter around while you are playing this game so that the kids can associate the letter with the sound.

Another simple oral game that will help familiarize kids with the initial sounds is a variation on the old "I Spy" game. The leader, either child, parent, or teacher, says, "I'm thinking of (or I spy) something in the room that starts with the letter______and which makes the______sound."

A more complicated oral game begins: "I'm going to Boston, and I'm taking an ant with me." The next player repeats what the first one has said and adds a word that begins with the *b* sound—"I'm going to Boston and I'm taking an ant and a banana." The third player continues, "I'm going to Boston and I'm taking an ant, and a banana, and a coat"...and so on, through the alphabet.

Another oral game that's a big hit is to have the kids recite a poem or sing a favorite song, substituting one sound for each initial sound in each word through the poem. For example, "Mary had a little lamb..." becomes "Bary bad a bittle bamb..." or "Harry had a hittle hamb..." or "Tary tad a tittle tamb...." For some reason, kids seem to find this exercise outrageously funny, especially if they manage to slip in a "swear word" or two. While we don't dissolve into helpless giggles each time we play it, we are pleased with how well it helps reinforce initial sounds. Sometimes we use a grab bag of Jumbo Alphabet letters and have the kids use the letter they've pulled out of the bag in their recitation. This way, the letter form and the sound are linked together in the children's minds.

Clap Down

This is another game that works well with kids who are always on the go and seem to learn best when they are in motion. Everybody sits in a circle, and the leader picks a letter and recites a list of words that begin with that sound. Each time the others hear a word that starts with that sound, they clap their hands. Once the group has coordinated this effort, the leader announces that the group is only to clap for that sound. Then the leader continues, slipping in a few words that don't start with the sound. For instance, the leader might say, "*b*, boy, box, barracuda, blimp, belly, peas." Inevitably, someone, to the accompaniment of knowledgeable giggles, claps for "peas."

We've tried eliminating the players who clap at the wrong time until we have a winner, but we've found that it works better just to play the game without concerning ourselves with winners and losers. When a parent and child are playing this game together, it can quickly degenerate into claps and laughter and giggles and roughhouse, which is fine.

Sorting Sounds

Materials:

13 sheets of shirt cardboard
scissors
marking pen

A set of objects or pictures representing each letter of the alphabet

Construction:

Cut your sheets of cardboard in half and print an upper- and lower-case letter on each sheet. If you like, cover the cardboard with clear contact paper for greater durability. If you want to make the game self-correcting, paste pictures of the objects that belong with each letter card on the back of the card.

Give the child the box of objects (or pictures) and ask him to place each object on the letter card that represents the sound that begins the name of the object. For instance, a pencil would go on the *Pp* card, a can on the *Cc* card, a ring on the *Rr* card.

Tracing and Copying Boards

Materials:

52 pieces of 4- by 3-inch tagboard
marking pen
clear contact paper
wipe-off crayons

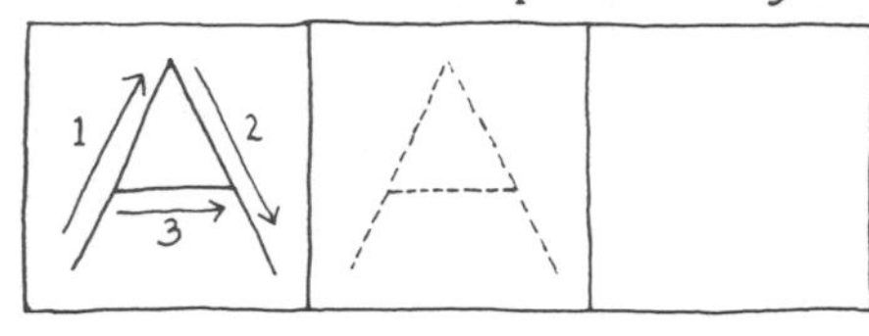

Construction:

Draw lines to divide each piece of tagboard into three equal sections. On the first section, write the letter and directional arrows to show how the letter is formed. On the second, outline the letter in dashes. Leave the third section blank for the children to write their own letters. Cover the entire piece with clear contact paper so the boards can be used over and over again. Use wipe-off crayons that wipe clean (regular crayons may leave marks). Eventually you may want to expand your set to include lower- and upper-case letters in both manuscript and cursive writing, and perhaps numbers as well. These boards are particularly useful for kids who are having difficulty tracing over and copying their Key Words. We usually give kids the letters from one of their Key Words to start. We show them how to form the letter following the arrows, then ask them to trace over the letter in the second section. Once they can do that, they can attempt to write it themselves in the blank section. Since the card can be wiped clean after each use, the cards can be used over and over again.

Cookie Letters

Materials:

2½ to 2¾ cups of flour
½ cup white or brown sugar
½ cup butter or margarine
1 teaspoon vanilla
2 eggs
2 teaspoons double-acting baking powder
½ teaspoon salt
measuring cups and spoons
mixing bowl
large spoons
cookie sheets

Construction:

Cream sugar with butter or margarine. Beat in vanilla, eggs, baking powder, and salt. Add flour gradually to form a stiff dough. Chill dough three to four hours. Then, divide the dough equally among the children and let them form letters. Bake the cookies at 375 degrees for 7 to 10 minutes on a greased cookie sheet. Makes thirty to forty cookie letters. All the kids enjoy this one and it will be especially useful to kids having trouble remembering and forming letters. As an extra treat, let them decorate the cookies with cake decorating gel once the cookies have cooled.

Clay Letters

Materials:

clay
a cookie sheet
glue
water
paint
paintbrushes

Construction:

The children create their own letters out of ceramic clay. Allow the letters to dry completely, then glaze them with a mixture of glue and water (half and half). Bake them overnight in the oven at the lowest possible temperature. When cool, the letters can be painted.

All the kids enjoy making their own ceramic alphabets. This activity is also useful for kids who are having difficulty remembering and making the letter forms. The tactile experience of rolling and shaping the letters helps impress the letter forms on their memories.

You can also use Play-doh or modeling clay to make clay letters. When you're finished, you won't be able to bake them, but the kids still get the tactile experience of forming the letters.

Blending

Here again, our kids get their first experience with blending when we go over their Key Words with them. After they have mastered the initial sounds, they can begin to blend these sounds together to form words.

When you are introducing the initial consonant sounds, try to cut the sounds short so you don't add a vowel sound to the consonant. For instance, try cutting the sound of the letter *C* off sharply without adding an extra "uh" sound so you are making just the hard *C* sound, not "kuh." Pay particular attention to *B, C, D, G, H, J, K, P,* and *T*, where this is liable to happen. Otherwise, you will end up with all kinds of extra sounds that will be confusing when you are introducing blending.

Two- and three-letter words are easy to blend; longer words are more difficult to sound out. Many phonics teachers make the mistake of asking a child to sound out a long word like *basket* by sounding out each letter one by one. Most kids get lost somewhere between the *s* and the *e* by this method. If you uncover one letter at a time and have the child pronounce all the letters uncovered thus far, you can avoid this problem. To make this a little clearer, let us give an example, using the word *basket*.

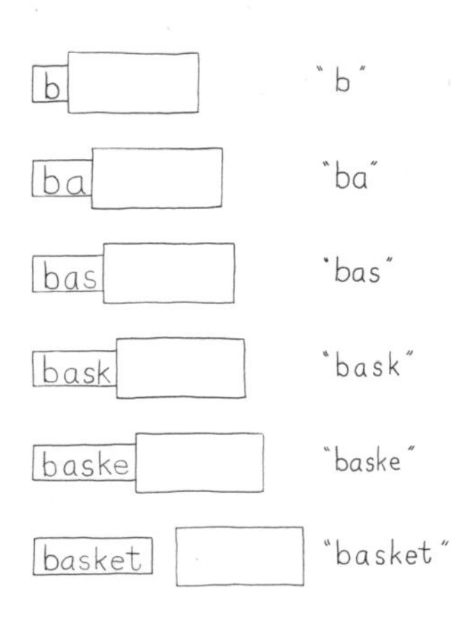

This is an important point, so if this explanation is puzzling, please spend a few moments figuring it out. It will make your attempt to teach phonics much easier.

Blending Dice

Materials:
3 square wooden cubes
(available at school
supply stores)
indelible marking pens

Construction:

On one cube, print the letters *a, e, i, o, u,* and *y*. On another cube print the letters *t, d, g, m, n, and p*. On the third cube, print the letters *b, r, s, c, m,* and *f*.

The first player picks up the dice and throws them. Then he tries to blend the sounds of the letters he has thrown to form a word. He may arrange the letters in any sequence. If he can blend his letters together to form a "real" (as opposed to nonsense) word, he gets to go again. If not, the next player takes a turn. The player with the most blended words wins. Score can be kept by writing the blended words under the player's name on a score sheet. Thus, the kids are practicing their writing skills at the same time they are learning about blending.

Word Families

Once the children have mastered the association of the letters of the alphabet with a particular sound and have gotten the hang of blending those sounds together to form words, we introduce them to a skill known in phonics circles as "initial consonant substitution" or, as we call it, Word Families. There are certain letter combinations that occur very frequently in our language. Take, for instance the letters *at*. By adding a consonant, say the letter *c*, we can make the word *cat*. By substituting other consonants, we can make the words *bat, fat, hat, mat, pat, rat, sat,* and *vat*.

The Word Family List in the Appendix will be useful for making the games described in this section.

Rhyming Sentences

Since words in the same word family rhyme with each other, we often make up rhymes for each family, like "I once had a rat who kept a fat cat under his hat; until, one day, he sat on the hat and that was that." Often, the kids will write or ask to have these rhymes written out for them and then illustrate them in book form.

Word Family Books

Materials:
construction paper
lined or unlined notebook paper
a stapler or a hole puncher and yarn
crayons, felt-tip markers, or paints

Construction:

Use the construction paper as a cover, and let the kids staple the pages together or punch holes and tie the book together with yarn.

We usually give the kids a letter combination, for instance, *op*, and then they write all the words they can make using *op*. They will sometimes write "nonwords" or "almost words" (as they call them) and will make up an illustration and definition for those words, too. It is important to check over these books carefully with the children. You may discover that a particular child will have written something like "san" and illustrated it with a picture of the beach. You'll need to help him hear the difference between "san" and "sand." Or you may find a child has made an *ed* word family book and has written "ded" and covered the page with tombstones, ghosts, etc. It is important to praise the child for the correct words and also to let him know that in our crazy language words are not always spelled the way they sound.

Word Wheels

Materials:
tagboard
scissors
marking pen

Construction:

Cut several circles, each approximately 5 by 6 inches in diameter, from your tagboard. Then cut three or four strips about 1 inch wide and 10 inches long. Print the alphabet in ¾-inch-high letters on the strips. In the center of the circle, cut two parallel notches about 1¼ inches long and 1 inch apart. Next to this, write a Word Family ending in ¾-inch-high letters. On the back of the word wheel, write all the possible words that can be made with the ending.

The children thread the alphabet strip through the slots. As they pull the strip, a different letter appears in front of each Word Family. The children can copy all the words they make on a sheet of paper. Then they can check their answers against the master list of possible answers on the back of the wheel. The kids also enjoy inventing new words and making up illustrations or definitions to go with them. (For instance: a "dat" is a cross between a cat and a dog.)

Word Family Go Fish or Concentration

Materials:
52 blank index cards
pens
colored contact paper (optional)

Construction:

To make this game more durable, we cover the backs of the index cards with colored contact paper. We usually make decks with fifty-two cards, because that's how many cards are in a regular card deck, but any number that is divisible by four will do. Select approximately thirteen Word Family endings from the Word Family List in the Appendix. Print one ending in the middle of each of four cards. Then print a word from that Word Family on each of four cards. For instance, you might choose the Word Family ending *ock* and write one of the words *clock, rock, sock, lock* on each card. For our younger or less sophisticated readers, we might also cut and paste or draw a picture representing the word.

The rules are the same as for the usual game of Go Fish (see pages 56–57), except that the player must ask for the card he wants by using the Word Family ending. For instance, he might say, "Do you have any *ock* words?" When he lays his cards down, the player reads his words to the others.

Word Family Concentration is played the same way as regular Concentration (see page 128); however, the players must read the words as they make up the pairs.

Long and Short Vowels

Children get their first experience with long and short vowels on their word cards. In the early games, we stress the short vowel sounds because they are more common in the short one-syllable words found in beginning reading.

Once the children have mastered the short vowels, we

introduce the concept of "long" and "short" vowels. We explain, for instance, that the letter *a* can make the short sound as in *cat* or the long sound as in *April, take, gate, make, rake,* etc., where the vowel "says" its own name. We don't introduce the formal and rather complex rules concerning long and short vowels to beginning readers. At this point, we're only concerned with their understanding that there are at least two different sounds for each vowel. And when they meet new words, they should try the long sound if the short sound doesn't blend into a recognizable word.

Vowel Chairs

Materials:
chairs, one less than the number of players

Construction:

Line the chairs up in two rows, back to back. This game is just a variation on the old party game Musical Chairs, where the players circle a row of back-to-back chairs and grab a seat when the music stops. Instead of music, the leader begins to chant a list of words that all have a particular long vowel sound: "tree, enormous, read, equal, thee. . . ." Then, when he says a short vowel word, such as *egg*, everyone scrambles for a seat. Each time there is one unseated player. This player withdraws from the game, taking a chair with him. If possible, make the withdrawing player the new leader and let him do the chanting.

Vowel Sort

Materials:

5 pieces of shirt cardboard or tagboard
blank index cards
old magazines
marking pen
scissors
glue

Construction:

Divide each shirt cardboard in half. On the top of one half of board, write a vowel with the marking to indicate that it is a short vowel (ă, ĕ, ĭ, ŏ, ŭ). On the other half, write the vowel with the mark to indicate a long sound (ā, ē, ī , ō ū).

Cut pictures representing words that have long vowel and short vowel sounds from magazines and glue them to the blank index cards. Write the word that the picture represents on the card. For instance, you might cut a picture of an apple, a gate, a plate, etc. for the ă/ā card.

To familiarize kids with the short and long sounds, give them a vowel board and the set of index cards and ask them to sort the cards onto the board, according to whether the pictured object has the long or short sound of the vowel. This game can be made self-correcting by writing the word *long* or *short* or drawing a long or short line on the back of the card.

Vowel Sounds in a Tube

Materials:

cylindrical cardboard
  container (the kind that
  potato chips come in)
paper liners from such cans
marking pens
scissors

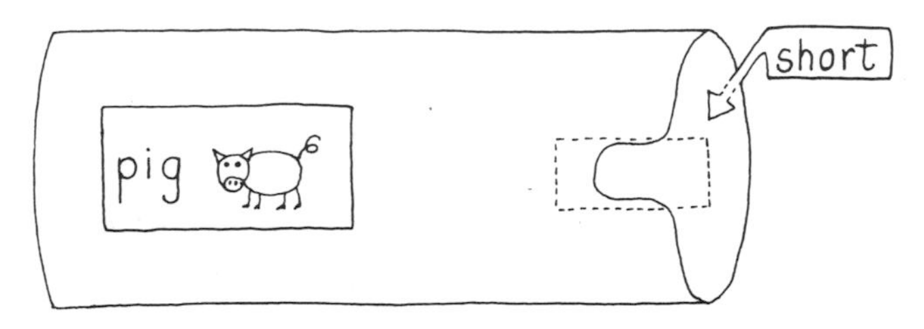

Construction:

Remove the paper liner from the cylinder and cut a window about 1½ inches wide and 1 inch long on one surface. Then roll the can around and cut an answer window of the same dimensions on the opposite side. Replace the liner, and you're ready to "program" your tube by drawing pictures and writing words with long or short vowels in the first window and the appropriate response (i.e., "long" or "short") in the opposite window. You can save liners from other containers and use this particular device for any number of self-checking practice skills.

The child turns the cardboard liner until he can see the picture and word in the front window. Then he decides whether the vowel is long or short. He marks his answer on a sheet of paper or simply turns the cylinder and checks his answer in the back window.

Silent E Game

Materials:

squares of clear acetate
blank 3- by 5-inch index cards
2 indelible marking pens of
  different colors
pictures cut from old
  magazines

Construction:

Print the letter *e* on each of several squares of acetate. Then, on the first set of blank cards, words selected from the Silent E Word List in the appendix. Print the words in the same style and size as your clear *e*'s, but in a different color. Leave enough room on each of these word cards for the addition of a clear *e*. On the second deck of cards, draw or glue pictures cut from magazines to represent words from the Silent E List. On the back of each of these cards, print the corresponding word.

We use this game to help children understand how the silent *e* works. The silent *e*, of course, is that tricky letter that appears at the end of one-syllable words having two vowels and causes the first vowel to have a long sound, or to "say its own name."

The materials you have made can be used in different ways. When introducing the concept, you might work individually with a child, asking him to pronounce the word printed on one of the word cards. Explain that the addition of our special silent *e* will change the word and make the first vowel have its long sound or "say its own name." Next, read a few examples. Then ask the child to place the silent *e* on one of the word cards and to pronounce it himself. The children can practice adding the clear *e* to the word cards and selecting the proper picture. The picture will aid the child in pronouncing the transformed word. This game can be worked individually or in groups. The word cards can be dealt out and the children can take turns matching word and picture cards.

Consonant Blends and Digraphs

A consonant blend is a combination of two or three consonants that are often found together in our language. Each letter makes its own sound, so a consonant blend can be sounded out letter by letter by a child with good phonic skills. Digraphs are a bit more difficult. A digraph is two or more consonants that make a single speech sound. Thus, they cannot be sounded out phonetically. Since consonant blends occur so frequently and digraphs have to be learned, we also use some games that help familiarize kids with these consonant combinations.

Many of the same games can be used for both blends and digraphs. Also, blends and digraphs can be taught as a single letter; thus, many of the games and activities for teaching the alphabet can be used to teach blends and digraphs. For instance, Alphabet Match-ups, Compact Alphabets, Sorting Sounds, and Clap Down can easily be expanded to include blends and digraphs. The Word Wheels game can also be adapted to include a strip of blends and digraphs. The Blends and Digraph word list in the Appendix will help you in selecting words to use when making these blend and digraph games.

Consonant Blends and Digraph Sort

Materials:

tagboard
blank 3 by 5-inch cards
pictures cut from magazines
glue
scissors

Construction:

Divide your tagboard into sections 6 by 5 inches. Write a consonant blend or digraph at the top of each section. Then paste or draw pictures of objects that have those letters on your blank cards. To make the game self-correcting, write the appropriate blend or digraph on the back of each card.

The children are given the set of the picture cards and the playing board and asked to lay the card on the appropriate section. Two or more players can use this game as well. Each player is dealt a stack of cards face down. On his turn, the player picks up a card and lays it on the correct square. The next player checks the first player's card. If it is correct, it remains on the square and the player scores a point. Play continues until all the cards are played. Player with the highest number of points wins.

Blends and Ends Dice

Materials:
2 square wooden cubes (available at school supply stores)
marking pen

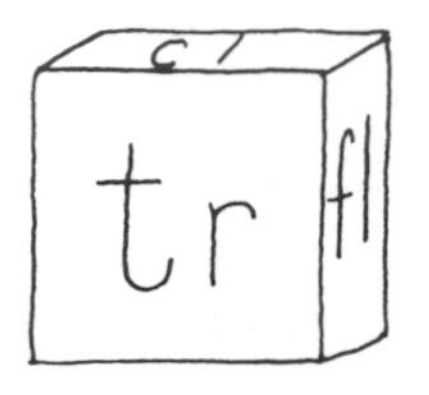

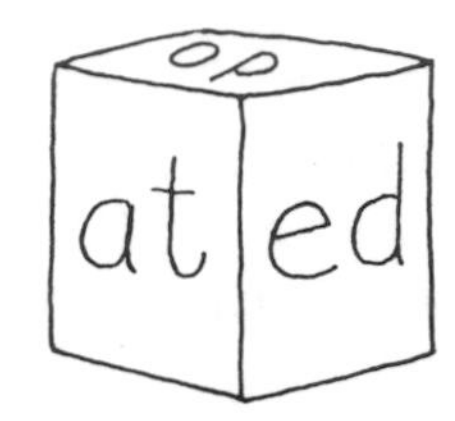

Construction:

On one of the die, write a consonant blend on each face. Choose any six of the following: *tr, cl, fl, bl, cb, sn, sk, sp*. On the other die write common Word Family endings. Choose any six of the following: *ip, op, ap, ed, in, ot, um, ag, at, ug*.

The players take turns rolling the dice. If the player can blend a "real" word from the letters he has thrown, he scores a point and gets to go again. If not, he loses his turn. Any player may challenge the word pronounced. If the challenged player cannot define his word or use it in a sentence, he loses his point to the challenger and the next player takes his turn.

Beyond Introductory Phonics

Although we may work on more sophisticated phonics rules with our advanced readers, this is usually to help them more with their spelling than their reading. The advanced phonic rules generally cover the vowel sounds, which have a tremendous amount of variation. Vowels do have other sounds besides long and short, but exceptions to the rules governing these other vowel sounds are almost as numerous as the rules themselves. The Appendix at the end of this book summarizes these rules. Although most beginning readers do not need to learn these rules per se, you may find that reading through them will help you understand the vowel sound variations a bit better and thus enable you to explain them to children if questions should arise.

Whole-Word Games

The following games are based on the whole-word method of teaching. These games are particularly effective in helping familiarize kids with words that don't conform to phonic rules. They will also help kids learn words that are not usually chosen for Key Words, but are used in their own stories and in the books that they eventually read.

The Appendix includes a Basic Vocabulary List of primary-grade-level reading words. The list is useful because it is based on frequency of usage (how often the word is used in written language). If you want to try some of the games and activities described below, this list can be very helpful.

Literary Go Fish

Materials:
52 blank index cards
scissors
marking pen
colored contact paper (optional)

Construction:

To make the cards more durable and more attractive, you can cover them with brightly colored contact paper. Generally we use fifty-two cards per deck, but this is an arbitrary number. Any number that's divisible by four will do. Next you will want to select categories of words. For instance, you might choose birds, fish, insects, mammals, trees, flowers, plants, and the like. Divide your cards into sets of four and print the name of each category at the top of the cards in each set. Then, depending on how sophisticated your readers are and what they are ready to handle, you print the name or draw a picture of an object (or do both) that fits into that category. For instance, your bird cards might include a robin, a sparrow, a hawk, and an eagle.

The rules are the same as those for regular Go Fish (see page 56–57). The players request cards from other players by categories. As each player lays down his cards, he reads them to the other players.

Word Concentration

Materials:
52 blank index cards
marking pens
colored contact paper
(optional)

Construction:

Select thirteen words from the Basic Vocabulary List (see Appendix). Print each word on four different cards. To make the set more durable and attractive, you can cover the backs of your cards with colored contact paper. We make several decks for classroom use, starting with the thirteen simplest words and working up to more difficult ones.

The cards are set out face down and the first player turns over two cards. If they match (have the same word on them), he gets to keep the two cards and take another turn. If they don't match, he replaces them face down in the same spot and the next player takes his turn. Play continues until all the cards are matched up. We encourage, but don't insist, that the children pronounce the words as they turn them over. Pairing an older child and a younger one together for this game works well, since the older one will tend to mumble things like "Let me see, where was that other *them* card?" Thus, the younger one will pick up a number of new words.

Basic Vocabulary Bingo

Materials:

5 sheets of tagboard approximately 8½ by 11 inches
approximately 20 blank index cards
poker chips
marking pen
ruler

WORD BINGO					
ACT	BAG			MAY	
VERY		US	CAR	BALL	
		BE		SHE	DO
					IN
CAME	SAID		IT	WITH	
		WERE	FAR		

Construction:

This game can accommodate up to five players. If you want more children to be able to play at once, simply increase the number of sheets and of index cards. Our first bingo sheets are divided into nine squares. Later on, we make the game more complex by dividing the cards into sixteen or more squares.

Select a group of words from the Basic Vocabulary List in the Appendix. Print one of these words on each of your blank index cards. Then print these words at random on the squares of your tagboard sheets.

To play the game, the caller, usually a teacher, parent, or more advanced reader, holds up one of the index cards and reads the word printed on it. If that word appears on a player's card, he may cover it with a poker chip. Sometimes, we decide that the first player to cover a complete row horizontally or vertically wins. At other times, we'll require the players to cover all the words on their cards with poker chips in order to win.

Occasionally, a child wants to be the caller even though he can't read all the words. That's fine—he can hold up the cards and let someone else read them. The particular rules and mechanics aren't important. The kids aren't having a lesson, they're playing a game. You're just sneaking a little learning in on the side.

Scrambled Words

Materials:
strips of paper
envelopes
scissors
marking pen

Construction:

Select a group of words from the Basic Vocabulary List at the end of this book. Print each word on a strip of paper. Cut the strips into pieces so that there is one letter on each piece. Store the letter pieces of each word in a separate envelope.

The idea is for the child to take the set of envelopes and to spell a word out of the letters in each envelope. One variation on this game that our kids enjoy is writing their own names on a strip of paper, cutting the strips, and putting the pieces into an envelope. Next we collect the envelopes, shuffle them, and let each child pick an envelope. Then each kid tries to unscramble the letters and spell the name. It's not too long before everyone in the group knows how to read and spell everyone else's name.

Word Collages

Materials:
old magazines
scissors
glue
cardboard or tagboard

Construction:

The kids cut words out of magazines and glue them to cardboard or tagboard to create a collage. This can be done individually or by a whole group of children working together to create a giant Word Collage.

After the kids have created their collages, assign tasks like: "Make a list of all the words that start with the same sound"; "Make a list of rhyming words for some of the words in your collage"; "Find the shortest word or the longest one"; "Read the words out loud"; and so on.

Labels

Materials:

Plastic-label maker or blank index cards
marking pens
tape

Construction:

The plastic-label makers that come with rolls of peel-off, sticky plastic tape are a great favorite with kids. They turn the dial to select a letter and squeeze the handle of the label maker to emboss a letter on the plastic tape. Or you can make labels by simply printing on index cards. The Printing Block Letters described on page 104 are also excellent for making labels.

Help the child to make a set of labels of common household or classroom objects. Then let him tape the labels in the appropriate places—the "toilet" label on the toilet, "phone" on the telephone, and so forth. To start, you might limit the game to one or two labels and then make new sets from time to time.

Name Cards

Materials:

Blank cards, one for each child in the class
marking pen
box for storage

Construction:

Print each child's name on a card in large letters. Label your storage box "Here."

When we take attendance in our classrooms, we do it by holding up each child's name card. If the child is present, he comes up and takes his card and puts it in the "Here" box. At first, we say the child's name when we hold up the card, but as the child learns to recognize his printed name, we merely hold the card up. It's not too long before the children learn to recognize each other's names.

Wish Books

Materials:

mail-order catalogs
looseleaf notebook binder
blank sheets of paper
scissors
glue
marking pens

Construction:

The kids can make these Wish Books all by themselves. They can leaf through the catalogs and pick out their favorite items. Then, with scissors and glue, they do their "shopping" and fill up their wish books. At the top of each page, they print the name of the item, and then paste the picture underneath. Later on, they may cut out the catalog description and the colors, sizes, etc., that they choose as well. Filling out order blanks from the catalog is another Wish Book activity that works well with more experienced readers. Families can have a lot of fun filling up Wish Books. Around holiday time, assign your child the job of making up a Wish Book for family members and friends. The child gets the experience of interviewing people, adding lots of new words to his vocabulary, and practicing his writing—and you might find this book a handy aid when shopping for gifts.

Scavenger Hunt

Materials:

10 to 20 index cards
marking pens

Construction:

Write the names of small, movable objects that can be found in the classroom, home or play yard. Have the kids break up into two or more teams. Give each team a set of word cards with the names of the small objects. The idea is for them to hunt for the various objects. The first team finished reads their cards and displays their objects to the second team and vice versa. Kids enjoy this game and usually manage to add a few words to their sight vocabulary as well.

Coupon Cards

Materials:

"money-off" advertising coupons
blank index cards
paste
colored contact paper (optional)

Construction:

Make a collection of coupons and paste them on the index cards. To make the deck more durable, you can back the cards with brightly colored contact paper. Make a master list of all your coupons. You might want to separate those coupons which have a picture of the product from those that are all text. Use the picture coupons for the less sophisticated readers and the all-text ones for advanced readers.

To begin, deal out the coupons to the players. The caller reads a product at random from the list. If a player has the coupon, he may "redeem" it by turning it in to the caller. If he turns in a wrong coupon, he has to take his coupon back as well as an extra one from the reserve pile. The first player to get rid of all his coupons wins.

Parents might let their children sort through magazines and newspapers and cut out coupons for products that the family uses. Then the child can turn them in at the grocery store and keep the money saved. Your children probably won't get rich doing this, but they become wonderfully adept at reading product names. The only problem you might run into is convincing your child that the family doesn't need a box of the latest brand of chocolate marshmallow–flavored dog biscuits.

Body Parts

Materials:
tape
index cards
marking pens

Construction:

Print, or have the children print, the words for different parts of the body on the word cards. One player tapes the index cards to the other's body in scramble order. For instance, the "head" card might be taped to the knee, the "nose" card to the foot, and so on. The other child or children must unscramble the cards and tape all the labels in the proper place. This game usually gets pretty giggly, but it's amazing how quickly the kids will learn to recognize the body-part words.

Word Walk

Materials:
pads of paper and pens

This activity gets the kids outdoors and lets them know that reading doesn't just happen in books. Armed with pads and pens, we walk around the block compiling lists of words we see on signs: "Stop," "One Way," "Freeway," "For Sale," "Gas," "Eat," "Slow School Crossing," "Yield," "Hotel," "Beware of Dog," and so forth.

When we get back, we sit down with our lists and pore over them. We might ask a child or a group of children to find all the words that begin with the same letter or sound or to find the shortest word, the longest word, or a word no one else has on his list. Maybe we'll write a story about the adventure using the words we've found; or we might ask each child to separate his words into lists according to words that have to do with food, cars, laws, animals, etc. We encourage kids to copy words even if they cannot read the words. When we go through the lists, we ask each child to separate his words into those he knows and those that are new to him. Then we ask them to find someone who will help them read those words. Finally, we ask the children to find partners and read these new words to each other. It's a noisy activity, with lots of conferring back and forth, and it's also a great learning activity.

The games, activities, and exercises in this chapter have proven to be valuable teaching aids for us. They can provide a strong background in phonics and help children build a basic sight-word vocabulary. They serve as a supplement to the Key Word Cards and Stories and help prepare kids for the next step in the Key Word Process and for journal writing, which is described in the next chapter.

6

OVER THE HUMP

Not long ago, we had an experience in a ballet class that reminded us of something that happens with kids who are learning to read. We were practicing an intricate turn—head poised, feet placed just so, body in balance, and eyes fixed on some distant point. Over and over again, we practiced a multitude of dizzying, stumbling turns without any noticeable improvement until, suddenly, for no reason at all, we were twirling lightly and gracefully around the room, each turn smoothly and perfectly executed.

The same kind of thing sometimes happens with kids and reading. It's like an explosion, a quantum leap. The children will be reading their Key Words, short, three- and four-letter words, awkwardly printing letters, and laboriously sounding out new words. Then, somehow, the next time you turn around, they're reading new words without even sounding them out. No longer content to dictate stories, they grab the pen out of your hand and begin to write the stories themselves. They're reading rapidly and smoothly picking up books and whipping right through them. Of course, it's not always like this, but more often than not, children do make this seemingly overnight progress and transformation. It always amazes us, and we're never quite sure what's happened. Something just seems to click into place and they're off. They're over the hump!

Journals

Most children make the transition from dictating stories to journal writing at this over-the-hump stage. Once they've had a

good deal of experience in dictating stories to us, we dispense with the Key Word cards. Their phonic skills and sight-word vocabularies are fairly well developed by this point. They can form all the letters of the alphabet by themselves. They can tell a logical, coherent story, and they trust us and themselves enough to tell stories that are full of personal meaning. The Key Words are therefore no longer necessary.

After they have dispensed with the Key Words, we try to make a careful assessment of each child's abilities. If they need more work in certain areas (phonics, sight words, letter formation), we make sure that they have plenty of opportunities to strengthen those skills in preparation for journal writing.

The transition from dictating Key Word Stories to writing stories all by themselves often occurs quite spontaneously. Many children literally grab the pen out of our hands. "I want to do it myself" is a familiar cry in our classrooms.

Of course, some children are a bit more cautious. In this case, once we think that they are ready, we'll invite them to try their hand at writing the story themselves. The first time the children take the pen in hand, they don't usually write the whole story. At first, they might just write a word or copy a line or two at the end of their story.

I was walking down the sidewalk and with my friends and then I came to this house. And when I was walking up to the door this dressed up person was dressed up as a gorilla. All my friends got scared 'cause

The next time they might begin the story, sitting close to us for consultation and reassurance. It often happens in the early stages of this transition between dictated stories and journal writing that, although the child will start the story, it will be too much for him to finish. In this case, we'll take over and write the end of the story he is telling.

At first, the children sit right next to us while they're writing. We're there to reassure them about spelling, punctuation, and other details. However, in these first stages, we don't offer corrections unless we are asked. Correcting children at this point would be disruptive. There are inevitably a lot of mistakes—misspellings, incorrect grammar, punctuation, or capitalization, letter reversals, improper spacing between words, barely legible handwriting, and the like. But, we don't bother about that in these first few stories.

We often notice a sort of regression at this stage. Handwriting deteriorates; words that have been spelled correctly in the parts of the stories they have written themselves are now spelled incorrectly; letters are reversed. Perhaps this is due to a certain nervousness. This is, after all, something new and different, and the children are not quite sure of themselves. Or perhaps it is because the stories are really their own now—not filtered through the hand of an adult. So much of their attention is now given to putting down the thoughts, to what is being said, that there just isn't enough left over to note such details. This is perfectly O.K.; the details of spelling, punctuation, and handwriting will come later, after they're comfortable with this new step.

Even after the children have worked on their journals for a good while, we may still be called upon from time to time to take dictation. A child may have a story to tell that is just too long, too complex, or too urgent for him to handle by himself. So, once again, we sit down together and write the story the child gives us. Or sometimes they'll just want to return to the old way of doing things, and ask us to write the story for them.

The independent journal entries are usually a combination of diary-type stories and stories like those that appeared in the Key Words books.

Once we feel that the children have sufficient confidence and skill to write their journal entries without us hovering about, we quietly and without fanfare make our exit, leaving them to their own devices. There's no point in announcing: "Today I want you to do it all by yourself." Certainly birds are much more clever about pushing their young out of the nest. They simply do it. Thus, we take advantage of the inevitable interruption and say, "You go on with the story now while I. . ." Then, of course, we reappear to have the story reread to us. Parents, too, can undoubtedly find a thousand such excuses to remove themselves from the journal writing and start their children on the road to independent writing.

When children have finished writing and, if they choose, illustrating their journal entries, we make a point of rereading them. Sometimes, the child will reread the story; at other times, we will. Often, when the story is reread, children will notice and correct their own mistakes.

After we've managed to push our young writers out of the nest for the first time, they generally continue their journal writing independently. We are still available as technical consultants in matters of punctuation, grammar, and spelling. Generally, except for occasional support and encouragement, it is no longer necessary for us to sit right next to them.

If a child feels too overwhelmed by the task of writing the story all by himself, we may insert an extra step. We will write down the dictated story on a separate piece of paper, and then the child will recopy the story in his Key Word Book. This extra step helps reassure kids that they can indeed write a story all by themselves.

The biggest difficulty we have in getting kids to make the move from dictated stories to independent writing is their fear of misspelling. Children are often very fussy about spelling at this stage. Perhaps this is because they want their creations to be as perfect as possible. Peer pressure is also a factor here. The children often trade journals and show off their stories to each other. There is probably no more haughty disdain than that shown by a seven-year-old informing a six-year-old that "*dumb* is spelled *d-u-m-b* not *d-u-m*, dummy!" Then too, the intricacies of spelling our nonphonetic language can be rather intimidating. The plaintive cry "What if I don't know how to spell a word?" often accompanies our attempts to push young writers into independent writing.

We explain to the children that we will help them make corrections when we reread the journals with them. Thus, although we ourselves are not terribly concerned with "correctness" in these early stories, many childen are. Even with children who are not at all concerned about spelling errors, these sorts of errors are the first ones that we correct. We try to wait until the children have gotten comfortable with journal writing and have written several entries before we begin to deal with spelling mistakes. If a child repeatedly misspells the same word, we draw his attention to it right away, for writing a word the wrong way only serves to reinforce the mistake and to make it harder to correct.

Next, we concentrate on capitalization, punctuation, and grammar. If a child has misspelled words, improperly used capital letters, written run-on sentences, and had other grammar problems all in the same story, we don't try to correct everything at once. One or two corrections per journal entry is enough. We don't want to discourage our young writers. Nor do we make corrections by marking up their journals with red ink (or any other color, for that matter). We simply point out the mistakes and let the child erase or cross out and correct his own mistakes. Our writing in his journal without being invited to would be looked upon as a great rudeness. The journals are the children's personal property. We would no more think of writing on them than we would of writing in a library book.

Gradually, we begin to introduce lined paper, so that the children can improve their handwriting. We use ruled primary paper, which has widely spaced lines, so that the kids have lots of room for their letters. Our first concern is to get the often wandering lines of print to conform to a straight line. Then we concentrate on uniform size, neatness, and proper spacing between words. Generally, children are quite proud of their journals and eager to make them more presentable, so they are quite pleased by the introduction of the lined paper.

Cursive Writing

Many of the children get interested in cursive writing at this point. Cursive writing or handwriting, as it is often called, is a much older form than manuscript writing, or printing. The latter is actually a fairly new innovation. The manuscript system was developed in England in 1914 and was used widely in English schools in the early 1920s. The system grew in popularity because it was considered easier to learn, being built on a simple system of sticks, circles, and partial circles. Also, the letter forms are similar to those in most printed books. By the 1930s, it became common in most American schools.

The chief advantage to cursive writing is that it is a much faster way to write. Most schools don't introduce cursive until the second or third grade, or even later. Many kids get interested earlier than that, probably because they consider it "grown-up" writing. Actually, the letter forms are similar enough that it is not too difficult to move from one system of writing to the other. Take for instance, the lower-case letters.

a b c d e f g h i j k l m n o p q r s t u v w x y z

abcdefghijklmnopqrstuvwxyz

Only *k, r, s, and z* are really much different. The transition from one style of writing to the other, then, doesn't usually present any big problems. We show kids the cursive alphabet and compare it with the manuscript letters they already know. We also make cursive letter boards, just like the ones we make for manuscript writing, with arrows indicating the pattern used in forming the letters. See "Tracing and Copying Boards," page 114. Practicing with the boards helps familiarize kids with the cursive alphabet.

Sometimes the kids practice cursive by dictating their journal entry, which we then write in cursive. They begin by tracing over our writing and then copying underneath all by themselves. Finally, they begin to write using cursive in their journals.

If I was a pony I would
love it because I would
be free. I would like
to run fast. It would
be real fun but
there is only one
problem because they
would put a holter
on me if they
Caught me.

by [illegible]

Reading Books

By the time the children have progressed to journal writing, they are quite well prepared to read "real" or adult-written books. Of course, many of our children get interested in commercial books long before they are writing in their journals. Generally, by the time they are dictating stories and have played the alphabet and Word Family games listed in chapter 5, they have enough reading skill to deal with beginning reading books.

Our favorite series of beginning readers is the Dr. Seuss Bright and Early Books and Beginner Books published by Random House. The vocabularies are simple, but interesting. Children are delighted by the fanciful characters and stories. The books introduce many of the same phonic rules that the children are developing in the games and activities described in the last chapter. One of the books from the series, *Hop on Pop*, for instance, introduces the *op* Word Family. We use these Bright and Early Readers with children who want to read real books once they've reached the story-dictating stage, and we highly recommend them to all parents and teachers.

The main thing that we do for our over-the-hump readers is to make sure that they have plenty of good books to read, books that are as meaningful and as fun to read as the stories they have written themselves. We spend a good deal of time selecting books and are lucky enough to have a marvelous librarian at our school whose guidance in selecting children's books is invaluable. With her help, we have compiled the bibliography that appears in the Appendix. It is by no means complete—it doesn't even contain all of our personal favorites—but we think it can be helpful for parents and teachers using the Key Word approach.

Because our children have learned to read and write using Key Words, a process that involves them emotionally as well as intellectually, they seem to enjoy and benefit from books that deal with feelings. Thus, our selection of children's books focuses on "tender topic" books that deal with subjects like death, old age, divorce, sibling rivalry, sex, birth, handicaps. We also include books that give a fair treatment of the sexes, books that deal with minority groups, and books that promise a sense of self-concept or self-worth.

In the last few years, there have been many wonderful books written on these topics. Not all such books are satisfactory in every way. Many have very serious flaws. Yet even the flawed ones are valuable, for they can touch off thought-provoking discussions.

Evaluating and Analyzing Stories

We spend a good deal of time discussing with the children the books that we read with them. We feel the children's ability to judge, criticize, and evaluate what they read is at least as important as the technical ability to read the printed word.

There are a number of different ways to approach discussing books with children. We often start by making a list of the characters. Who is the story mainly about? Who are the heroes? The villains? Who is on whose side? Whom do you like? Dislike? Why? Have you ever felt like the character in the story?

When we discuss what exactly the book was all about, we

might ask the kids to retell the story in their own words. If they are old enough, they can write a short summary of the story. This is an excellent way of developing comprehension and of getting kids to identify the main idea and the significant details in the books they read. We also ask the kids whether they think the story is fact or fiction. Is it a real story or did the author make it up? How do you know?

The plots of many children's stories involve a problem or series of problems faced by a main character or group of characters. The plot hinges on the decisions made or actions taken in response to their problem. When we discuss the story, we might try to identify what the problem in the story is and to outline what actions or steps were taken. Then, once we have identified a crucial action or decision, we ask the kids to dream up alternative actions. What else could the character have done in response to the problem? How would that have changed the story? For example, in the book *Annie and the Old One*, a little Indian girl named Annie is faced with the problem of death. Her grandmother is weaving a rug and tells Annie that this is the last rug she will weave because her life will soon be over. Annie, who doesn't want her grandmother to die, sneaks out each evening and unravels the weaving in an attempt to stop the inevitable. Finally, the grandmother tells Annie that she must no longer unravel the rug, that it is part of the great cycle of life for her to make the transition from life to death, that she is old and wants her rest.

We first talk about why Annie has unraveled the rug, delving into her motivations. Then we talk about what other things Annie could have done instead.

In addition to asking these kinds of questions, we have a couple of activities we use in the classroom to help kids analyze and evaluate what they've read. Parents will find that these exercises can easily be adapted for use at home.

Rewrites

One interesting exercise is to have the children rewrite or retell the story from another character's point of view. This is especially helpful with tender topics when there simply isn't a book that deals adequately with a particular aspect of the topic. Books about sibling rivalry, for instance, usually portray the youngest or the middle sibling in the most positive role. Older siblings, especially older sisters, are usually the meanies. The exceptions are books about a new baby. These are usually aimed at helping the older child deal with the feelings of rejection and jealousy by building his self-concept. But generally, the youngest siblings are more positive characters. Thus, we might ask the children to rewrite or retell the story from the older sibling's or from the baby's point of view.

It can also be very useful to do this exercise with a story about divorce. There are a number of good books that deal with divorce, with the feelings of guilt and loss the child experiences, and with adjustments in life style like changing homes and schools and the absence of one parent in the home. But there is no book that talks about the guilt, anger, hurt, and difficult adjustments that the parents face. Asking children to retell a divorce story from one of the parents' point of view helps fill this gap and is an excellent exercise for them.

When we talk about books we've read, we often discuss the ending. Did you like the ending? Why or why not? Could the story have ended differently? If these questions touch off a conversation, we might ask the children to rewrite the story with a different ending.

Change the Characters

Once we've talked about the characters in a book, we might change them around a bit. For instance, we might make all the characters a different race, or change the sex or the age of the hero. Then, if possible, we retell or reread the story. How do these changes affect the story? Is the story more powerful or better? Does it lose something or make less sense when the characters are changed? Do you like the story better before or after the changes? Why?

Or we might change the physical appearance of the main character. The ugly monster might become handsome or the beautiful princess, ugly. How would you feel if the princess had warts all over her face and was ugly? Would you still like her or want to be like her? Would the other people in the story treat her differently? Could the same things have happened to her?

This changing of the characters can help kids understand how and why they respond to certain characters in certain ways. It can help them understand how sexism and racism can operate in literature and how an author's own prejudices are reflected in the books and stories they write.

Detective

Sometimes we play detective, pretending that it is our job to find out as much as we can about an author—such as the things he or she believes in and his or her life style and background—but the only clues we have are the book itself. Most children are familiar with this police technique of creating a speculative personality profile from a few clues, thanks to the endless string of detective shows on TV.

First of all, we start with the facts. The name will usually tell us what sex the author is, but we look in the text itself for confirmation. After all, maybe the author's using a pen name. If we have a story full of details about football with only boy characters, our detective squad might guess the author is a man because, as one kid put it, "In the olden days, girls didn't play football."

The publishing data in the front of the book are helpful. The copyright date will tell us when the book was written. If the book was published in another country, this might help us guess where the author lives.

The story itself might help us make some educated guesses about the author's background. If, for instance, a story is full of details about a particular area of the country, we might guess that the author lives or once lived there. Or, if the book discusses something in great detail, we might decide that the author has a particular interest in that subject. For instance, one story we read had a lot of information about commercial bee hives and honey. We guessed that the author's hobby might be beekeeping.

We might ask ourselves certain questions about the narrator or the author. Who is telling the story? How does the person who is telling the story want you to feel? Why did the author write this story? How did the author feel when writing the story? What does this tell us about the author as a person?

If an author has written a book on a tender topic, we try to figure out the attitudes the author has or the way he feels about the subject matter. Thus, in considering the author of a book on death, we might try to figure out whether the writer believes in God or in an afterlife. Or, if divorce is the topic, we might try to decide whether the author has ever experienced divorce.

If the author is also the illustrator of the book, the drawings can also give you clues about the kind of person the author is. For instance, one child pointed out that a certain author who wrote books about children living in the city always made the city look like a rather scary place. This suggested a certain attitude about the city as a place to live. Some children thought it meant that the author didn't like the city, so he wouldn't live there. Others thought that he lived in the city but that he hated city life.

We usually get a lot of information for our profile out of books featuring "mother-the-mop," exclusively ethnic families living in ghettos, and other stereotypes. Such stereotypes, or lack of them, will usually tell us a good deal about the author's attitudes.

Once we've finished our detective work, we try to verify it using reference books. There are a number of books that list authors and include a short bibliographic summary. You can even write to the author in care of the publisher explaining what you've done and asking him to verify your detective work. Most authors are delighted to get such letters, and the replies are always interesting.

Making Books

In addition to adult-written books, the children also read books that they themselves or their friends have written. A special section of our school library is devoted to the books that the children have written, illustrated, and bound themselves. The books are cataloged and coded and can be checked out just like the other books in the library.

The books that the children write cover a wide variety of subjects. There are collections of poems, riddles, and recipes; and books on the care of pet hamsters, wiring an electric light, making a fishing fly. There are books on divorce, on death, on friendships and fights, and the children are enormously proud of them.

Big Books

The topics for the books are usually the children's own ideas. Occasionally, though, we will make "Big Books," which are a collection of stories around a central theme that a group of children put together themselves. Sometimes the topics for Big Books arise out of our group discussions about the books we read or, rather, their shortcomings. Once, for instance, we had been reading a number of books about old age. The children felt that the old people in the stories and books we read were unrealistically inactive. Many of the children talked about their own grandparents, who jogged, ran their own businesses, played in orchestras, taught craft classes, etc. They didn't just sit in rocking chairs. So we decided to make our own book called *Out of the Rocking Chair*. Even children whose grandparents were no longer living got into the act. Once everyone had written or dictated his or her story, we pasted them into one of the oversized scrapbooks we use for these collections (hence the name Big Books). Then everyone decorated the page with his or her story. One little boy who had never known his grandmother wrote a delightful fantasy about a gang of construction-worker grannies who built tall skyscrapers.

Another favorite topic for Big Books is embarrassing moments. We usually start the ball rolling by telling the children some embarrassing moment of our own, like the time we had to go to the bathroom but the teacher didn't give us permission. (The fact that we once had to have permission to go to the bathroom astounds our children, who are used to simply getting up and going when the need arises.) We were, needless to say, quite embarrassed about peeing on the floor. To top it off, when we got to school the next day, someone had left a wrapped

package on our desk—a cork! The children love these stories about things that happened to us when we were children, and once we've told something embarrassing, they're ready to open up with stories on their own.

Book Binding

The special books that the children write require something more elaborate than the simple notebook binders or stapled-together pages that they use for Key Word Stories and journals. We've collected a number of different methods for binding books.

The easiest books to bind are the ones with soft covers. There are two basic methods for binding soft-cover books. The first, Japanese book binding, is quite simple. Even very young children can turn out an attractive book without adult help.

First cut two covers out of poster board the same size as the page you want to bind. Then use a ruler to draw a line on one of the covers about ½ inch from the edge you want to bind. Mark dots about ½ to 1 inch apart along this line, as in illustration 1.

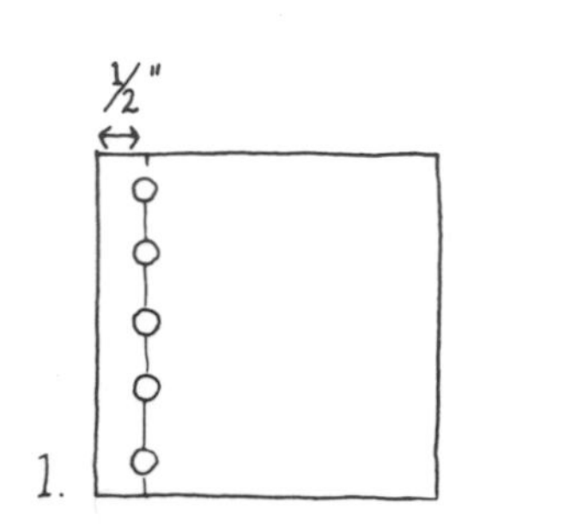

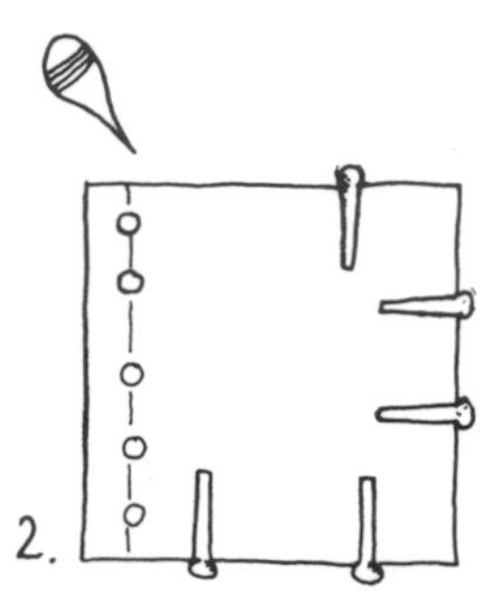

Slip the pages in between the two covers. Make sure all edges are even, and clip the covers and pages together with clothespins to keep them from slipping while you work. Punch holes at the dots with an awl or any poking tool, as in illustration 2.

Thread a strand of yarn or embroidery floss through the first hole, wrap it over the top, and thread it through the first hole again, leaving an inch or two of loose thread. Then pull it through the second hole, wrap it around the edge, and bring it back through the hole again. Continue this procedure until you have threaded the last hole (illustration 3). Bring the yarn or thread around the lower edge and go back through the holes again with a simple running stitch—in one hole and out the next. Wrap around the end. Cut the yarn and tie the loose ends together, as in illustration 4.

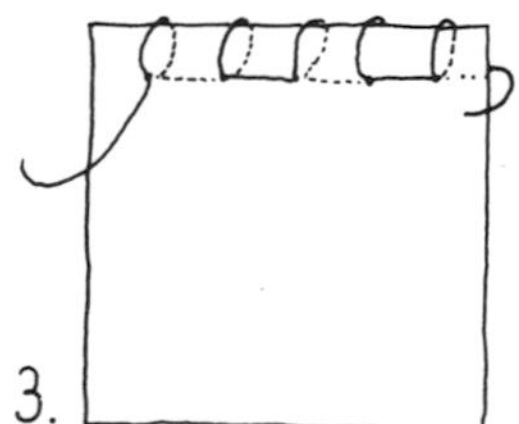

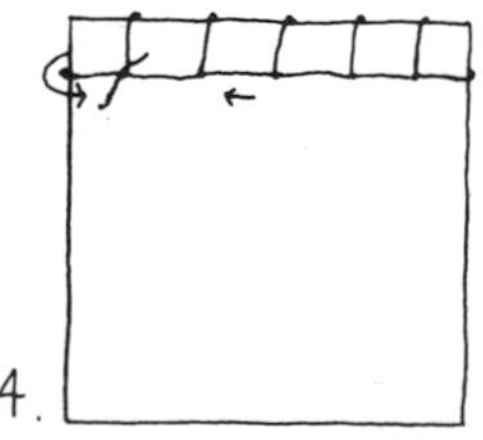

One of the most common forms of book binding is called signature binding. It's easy to sew if you don't try to do too many pages at once. You will need to cut a cover the same size as your paper, or slightly longer. Then fold both the paper and the cover

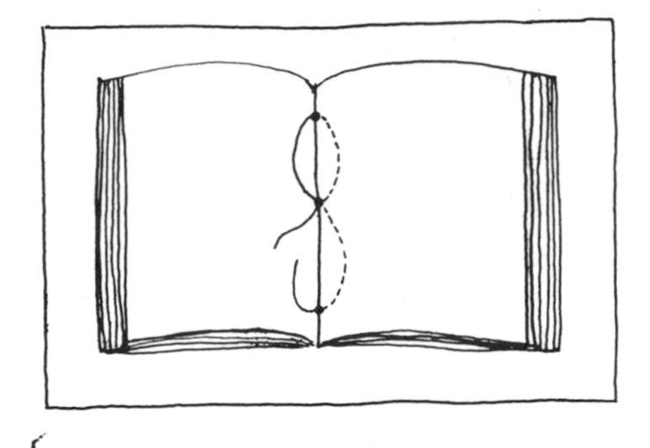

5.

6.

in half. Use a thick needle threaded with heavy-duty thread or thin nylon fishing line and sew along the fold in at least three places, as in illustration 5. Start sewing on the inside and tie the knot on the inside so that it won't show. If you want a smoother binding (for a hard cover), use more than three holes, as in illustration 6.

A group of signatures can be bound together to make a larger book, which can be covered with a decorative hard cover. First sew or tape the signatures together as shown in illustration 7.

Another way of joining pages together is to cut your paper and stack it evenly. Sandwich the edges you wish to bind between two rulers and hold them together with clamps. Prop the paper-bound edges up on two books (see p. 154).

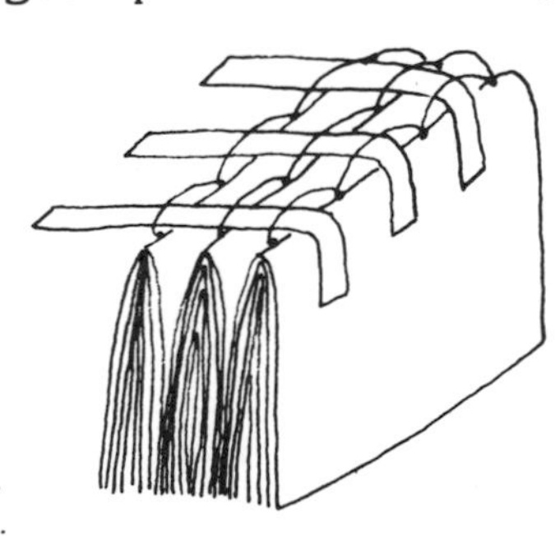

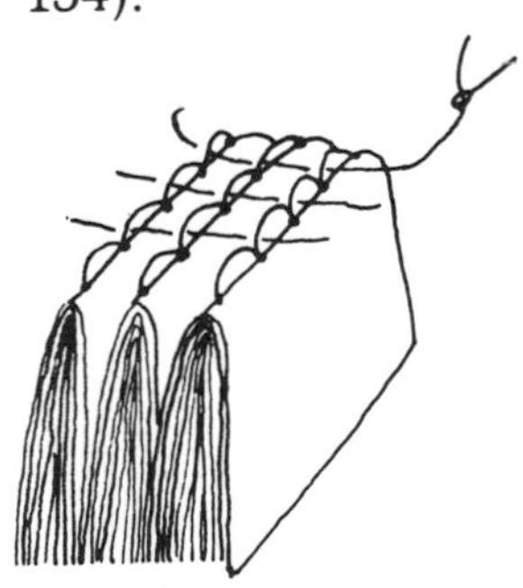

7.

Now bind the pages with a special type of glue. This glue, called padding compound, stays flexible when it dries so the pages will turn. It can be purchased from printer's supply outlets. Apply a coat with a paintbrush. Let it dry, and apply a second coat.

Once you have bound your pages, you can make a cover for your book. Almost any sort of paper or fabric can be used over cardboard to make a decorative cover. Papers with short fibers, like construction paper, tend to tear easily. Wallpaper or contact paper work well.

Fabric can also be used to cover books. However, unless it is handled properly, it becomes soaked with glue, gets splotchy, or buckles. You can eliminate most of these problems by lining the fabric with paper first. To laminate cloth to paper, spread a thin layer of white glue on a piece of newsprint or thin white paper. Smooth the paper onto the cloth.

To make your cover, cut two pieces of shirt cardboard about a quarter inch larger than your paper. Cut two pieces of wallpaper, wrapping paper, or fabric about 1 inch bigger than your cover on all sides. Using a glue stick or a paintbrush, cover the surface of your cardboard with white glue mixed with water. Smooth your decorative paper or fabric onto the cardboard. Cut or fold the corners.

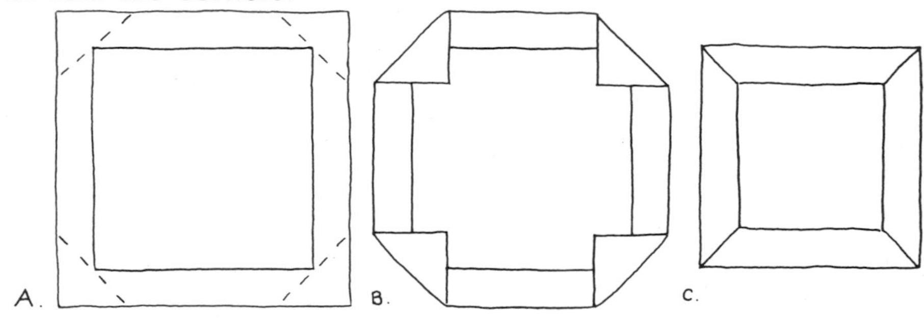

To join the cover and pages, you will need a strip of 1-inch-wide cloth tape the same length as your covers. Lay the strip of tape, sticky side up, on a flat surface. Lay the bound edge of your pages in the center of the tape so that the top and bottom edges of the cover are flush with the ends of the tape strip. Tape it up and down to secure the pages, and fold the tape over the front and back covers.

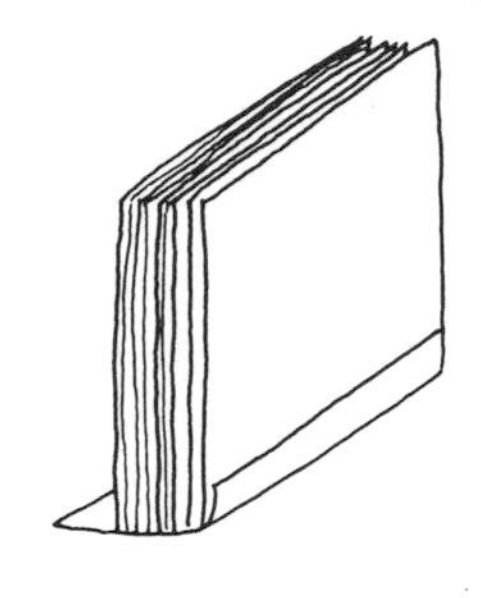

To finish, glue the first and last pages to the front and back covers as shown here. If you want to get fancy, you can cover the inside of the front and back covers with decorative end papers.

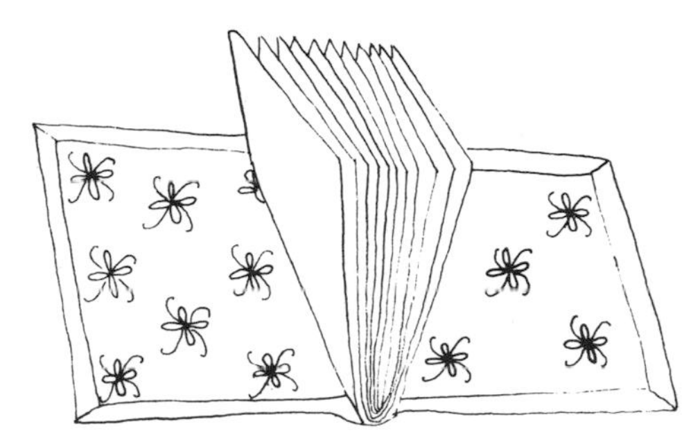

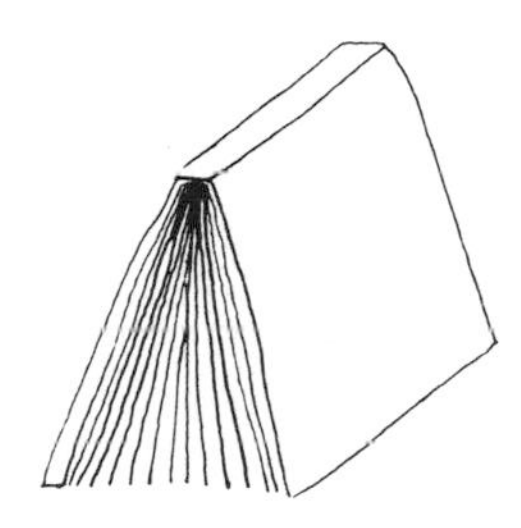

As we mentioned earlier, the main thing we do for our over-the-hump readers is to provide them with access to lots of interesting and varied books, both written by children and written by adults. The next section of this book contains an annotated bibliography of our favorite children's books that go beyond the usual sex and race stereotypes found in most children's literature and that deal with tender topics like sex, divorce, and sibling rivalry in a sensitive manner.

A number of more complete bibliographies of children's literature are available. Some of these are excellent and can be valuable aids for parents and teachers. The ones that we have found most useful are listed at the end of the bibliography.

APPENDIX

Annotated Bibliography of Children's Literature

Andry, Andrew C., and Kratka, Suzanne C. *Hi, New Baby: A Book to Help Your Child Learn about the New Baby*. New York: Simon & Schuster, 1970.

This book gives factual information about babies and talks about the feelings of anger and displacement experienced by older siblings. It suggests activities for older siblings that can help the baby, themselves, and the family in general. The book depicts both white and black families.

Baylor, Byrd. *The Desert Is Theirs*. New York: Scribner, 1975. *When Clay Sings*. New York: Scribner, 1972. *The Way to Start a Day*. New York: Scribner, 1978. *They Put On Masks*. New York: Scribner, 1974.

These and the other books by the same author are lyrical, poetic descriptions of Indian life. The quality of the language and the author's ability to communicate the spiritual values of Indian life have made these books award winners.

Bemelmans, Ludwig. *Madeline*. New York: Viking Press, 1939.

There is a whole series of books about the adventurous Madeline, who lives in a convent school in Paris. She is one of the classic nonstereotyped (well, almost) little girl heroes, and her adventures are still exciting today.

Brown, Margaret Wise. *The Dead Bird*. Reading, Mass: Addison-Wesley, 1958.

A very simple and beautiful story about a group of children who find a dead bird in the park. They hold a poetic childlike funeral and return to visit the site each day. . . until they forget. Reassures youngsters that it is O.K. to end your mourning and go on about your life.

Brown, Myra Berry. *Amy and the New Baby*. New York: Franklin Watts, 1965.

Amy has mixed feelings about her new brother, who cries too much, gets too much attention, and stays much longer than Amy had expected. The parents respond well, giving Amy special attention, letting her know their love has not diminished, but at the same time letting her know that the baby is now part of the family and is here to stay.

Byars, Betsy. *Go and Hush the Baby*. New York: Viking, 1971.

Brother Will has to baby-sit, though he'd rather go out and play baseball. Will ends up amusing both himself and the baby. His feeling of satisfaction of doing a job well and family warmth compensate for having to put off his desires.

Conklin, Gladys. *Journey of the Gray Whale*. New York: Holiday House, 1974.
A pod of whales migrates to Mexico, where a baby whale is born. The nurturing behavior of the midwife and mother whale plus the factual information about these gentle creatures makes this a valuable book.

Dragonwagon, Crescent. *Wind Rose*. New York: Harper & Row, 1976.
A lovely, lyrical story in which a mother describes to her child how the child was conceived, how it felt to carry the child inside her, and how the child's name was derived from the fact that the wind rose on the night of birth. A nurturing, loving story that, although it doesn't explain the sex act explicitly, puts forth the notion that sex is a beautiful, wonderful feeling.

Eber, Christine E. *Just Momma & Me*. Chapel Hill, N.C.: Lollipop Power, 1975.
The story of a little girl named Regina who is adopted by a single woman. When Karl, the boyfriend, moves in, Regina feels left out. When her mother becomes pregnant, Regina wishes that it could be like old times when it was "just Momma and me." When the mother leaves for the hospital, Karl and Regina develop a special friendship that helps Regina accept the idea that she can share love with the whole family, including her new baby brother. This book is valuable for the nonstereotyped family and sex roles as well as its approach to the new sibling.

Farrell, Sherrie. *Gabriel's Very First Birthday*. Seattle, Washington: Sherrie Farrell and Pipeline Books, 1976.
This very realistic book shows photographs of an actual birth. Although excellent, it is not the first book we use on birth since the pictures of the newborn baby emerging with blood on his body and of the cutting of the umbilical cord are sometimes frightening to children. It is important to supplement the text by talking about these pictures and reassuring children.

Feelings, Muriel. *Jambo Means Hello: Swahili Alphabet Book*. New York: Dial Press, 1974. *Moja Means One: The Swahili Counting Book*. New York: Dial Press, 1971.
These two beautifully illustrated books provide an introduction to the Swahili language and African culture.

Goldreich, Gloria, and Goldreich, Esther. *What Can She Be? An Architect*. New York: Lothrop, Lee & Shepard, 1974. *A Farmer*, 1976. *A Geologist*, 1976. *A Lawyer*, 1973. *A Musician*, 1975. *A Newscaster*, 1973. *A Police Officer*, 1975. *A Veterinarian*, 1972.
This series show women in a variety of nontraditional occupations. In addition to being nonsexist, these books offer children an idea of various occupations and the life styles they involve.

Gordon, Sol, and Gordon, Judith. *Did the Sun Shine before You Were Born?* New York: Third Press–Joseph Okpaku, 1974.

This sex education book for young children, one of the few available, is multiethnic and nonsexist and presents all sorts of families. It describes intercourse, pregnancy, and birth and is done in good taste.

Greenfield, Eloise. *She Come Bringing Me That Little Baby Girl*. Philadelphia: Lippincott, 1974.

Kevin is glad to see his mother come home from the hospital, even if she brings a sister instead of the brother he wanted. He starts to feel rejected when everyone fusses over the baby. Things look gloomy until he learns he can help care for the baby, as his uncle once cared for his mother. He feels comforted when he finds that one of his mother's arms is still available for him. Beautifully illustrated by John Steptoe.

Gripe, Maria. *The Night Daddy*. New York: Delacorte Press, 1971.

Set in Sweden, this book tells the story of the friendship between a girl and a writer who is hired to baby-sit at night while her mother works as a nurse. The nonstereotyped role models and the portrayal of single-parent family life make this a valuable book.

Hoban, Lillian. *Arthur's Christmas Cookies*. New York: Harper & Row, 1972. *Arthur's Honey Bear*. New York: Harper & Row, 1974. *Arthur's Pen Pal*. New York: Harper & Row, 1976.

These books are written simply enough to be read by a beginning reader. *Pen Pal* features Arthur, a young chimp, discovering that his pen pal, a karate-chopping, Indian-wrestling champion, is a "Sandra," not a "Sanford," which causes Arthur to think differently about his sister Violet and girls in general. In *Honey Bear*, Arthur holds a yard sale, but has trouble parting with his teddy bear. Finally, he sells it to his sister, who dresses it up as a girl. At first Arthur is horrified, then he decides he can be the bear's uncle and continue to hug and cuddle it. Despite the nonsexist approach, the illustrations always show girl chimps with aprons, dresses, and bows in their hair.

Hoban, Russell. *A Baby Sister for Frances*. New York: Harper & Row, 1964. *A Bargain for Frances*. New York: Harper & Row, 1970. *Bedtime for Frances*. New York: Harper & Row, 1960. *Best Friends for Frances*. New York: Harper & Row, 1969. *Birthday for Frances*. New York: Harper & Row, 1968. *Bread & Jam for Frances*. New York: Harper & Row, 1969. *Egg Thoughts & Other Frances Songs*. New York: Harper & Row, 1972.

Despite elements of sexism, these books still have value since they deal with emotional issues kids can relate to. For instance, in one story, Frances (a young badger) decides to run away when her new baby sister, Gloria, joins the family. She runs away, under the dining room table, and hears her parents talk about how much they miss her. The story is a child's fantasy come true: running away, thereby becoming the center of attention.

Hoffman, Phyllis. *Steffie and Me*. Illustrated by Emily McCully. New York: Harper & Row, 1970.

This is a warm story of two little girls who live in the same neighborhood, share adventures and have similar lives. Particularly valuable because of its portrayal of an interracial friendship, which is rare in children's books.

Hutchins, Pat. *Titch*. New York: Macmillan, 1971.

Titch is the youngest of three children. His brother and sister treat him well, but it is assumed that he can't do all the things his older brother and sister can. Everything he does is less important until he plants a seed that grows into a huge plant. An excellent book for siblings. The author also has several other nicely illustrated books with simple texts.

Ionesco, Eugene. *Story Number One*. New York: Harlan Quist, 1967. *Story Number Two*. New York: Harlan Quist, 1970. *Story Number Three*. New York: Harlan Quist, 1971. *Story Number Four*. New York: Harlan Quist, 1975.

These beautifully illustrated, surrealistic tales are as delightful for parents as they are for children. They can be confusing or mildly shocking, but above all, they are interesting and nonsexist to boot. The stories center on Josette and her loving, patient, imaginative father.

Kindred, Wendy. *Lucky Wilma*. New York: Dial, 1973.

This easy-to-read book tells the story of Wilma and her father, who comes to take her someplace special every Saturday. One day, when the museum is closed, they simply walk, run, and fantasize, which brings them closer than the usual planned visits. Deals with the "weekend daddy" syndrome and shows that children of divorced parents need not be miserable or cut off from one parent.

Kirk, Barbara. *Grandpa, Me and Our House in the Tree*. New York: Macmillan, 1978.

Story of a young child and a grandfather who build a tree house together. The grandfather gets sick and can no longer climb, but he still goes to the tree and sits in a chair while his grandchild climbs. A sensitive, realistic, and positive portrayal of aging.

Krementz, Jill. *A Very Young Dancer*. New York: Alfred A. Knopf, 1976. *A Very Young Gymnast*. New York: Alfred A. Knopf, 1977. *A Very Young Rider*. New York: Alfred A. Knopf, 1978.

These books describe the careers and life styles of three very talented young ladies. They are nonsexist and portray children as capable, achieving human beings.

Lasky, Kathryn. *I Have Four Names for My Grandfather*. Boston: Little, Brown, 1976.

A young boy named Tom describes his relationship with his grandfather. Not only is this book a warm, human portrait of a supportive, adult male, but it also portrays an aging person as competent and active.

Lionni, Leo. *Frederick*. New York: Random House, 1966. *Fish Is Fish*. New York: Random House, 1970.

These two are our favorites, but all of Lionni's books are excellent. In *Frederick*, we meet a mouse who is set apart from others who are busily storing up food and supplies for the long winter. It seems as if Frederick is doing nothing to help ensure the community's survival until one dreary day, when the food supplies are low and the winter seems endless, Frederick lifts the spirits of his companions with his tales of the colors and abundance of spring, sharing the memories he has stored up. Frederick, it turns out, is a poet.

Lobel, Arnold. *Frog and Toad Are Friends*. New York: Harper & Row, 1970. *Frog and Toad Together*. New York: Harper & Row, 1972. *Frog and Toad All Year*. New York: Harper & Row, 1976. *Owl at Home*. New York: Harper & Row, 1975.

Lobel creates "literature" using a first-grade vocabulary. These wise and entertaining stories are also charmingly illustrated. Among the best of the I-can-read books.

Mahy, Margaret. *The Man Whose Mother Was a Pirate*. New York: Atheneum Publishers, 1972.

A charming fantasy about a fussy businessman who leaves his workaday world behind and follows his disreputable pirate mother out to sea. Great illustrations and an interesting twist of roles.

Marshall, James. *George and Martha*. New York: Houghton Mifflin, 1972. *George and Martha Encore*. New York: Houghton Mifflin, 1973. *George and Martha Rise and Shine*. New York: Houghton Mifflin, 1976.

These stories center on two hippopotamuses named George and Martha. The short stories portray a loving, honest, and supportive friendship between a male and a female. A good model of friendship for children.

Maury, Inez. *My Mother, the Mail Carrier*. New York: Feminist Press, 1976.

This bilingual story is told by Lupita, the bright and energetic daughter of a mail carrier. The nonsexist portrayal of a single-parent ethnic family is entertaining and valuable.

McGovern, Ann. *Black Is Beautiful*. New York: Four Winds Press, 1969. *Runaway Slave*. New York: Four Winds Press, 1965.

The first book listed here has beautiful photos and a poetic text to help reinforce a positive self-image for blacks. The second book deals with the life of

Harriet Tubman, a courageous black woman who helped other slaves escape to freedom by the Underground Railway.

Merriam, Eve. *Mommies at Work*. New York: Alfred A. Knopf, 1961.

This classic picture book shows mommies at work in all different sorts of jobs. Written at a time when almost all females in children's books were mothers with mops, this book is still an important portrayal of roles for women.

Miles, Miska. *Annie and the Old One*. Boston: Little, Brown, 1971.

A little Navajo girl tries to prevent the predicted death of her grandmother. The book is an eloquent introduction to the idea of death as a natural part of the life cycle and not an event to be feared. One of the best books on death for children.

Mosel, Arlene. *Tikki Tikki Tembo*. New York: Holt, Rinehart & Winston, 1968. *The Funny Little Woman*. New York: Dutton, 1972.

Both books are retellings of Japanese folk stories. Children adore the first one because of the repetition. *The Funny Little Woman* has some of the most outstanding and subtle illustrations we've ever seen in children's books. Pay particular attention to the use of color and the progress of the drawings in the upper margins.

Ness, Evaline. *Sam Bangs and Moonshine*. New York: Holt, Rinehart & Winston, 1966.

Samantha, whose mother is dead, fantasizes quite a bit. Her fantasizing endangers the life of a friend, and Samantha learns the importance of distinguishing between what is real and what is not. A moral tale without being "preachy" and a portrait of a single-parent family headed by a man.

Newfield, Marcia. *A Book for Jodan*. New York: Atheneum, 1975.

This is our favorite book on divorce. It deals with the child's feeling of guilt and anger. The parents are both loving, supporting characters. Jodan misses her father after she and her mother move to California. On her visit back east, her father gives her a special book he has made that reassures her about his continuing love and conveys a philosophy that will help Jodan face and deal with the changes in her life.

Scott, Ann Herbert. *Sam*. New York: McGraw-Hill, 1967. *On Mother's Lap*. New York: McGraw-Hill, 1972.

Sam, the youngest member of a closely knit black family, approaches each member of the family wanting to help or participate in what they're doing. Everyone sends him off, but when he weeps in frustration, they all rally around, offering support. An important portrait of a black family, of the feelings of younger siblings, and of a little boy dealing with his emotions.

The second book also deals with families, and with sibling rivalry. Michael and his family are Eskimos, but we know this only because of the text. Mother makes it clear that there is room for everything and everyone. Her lap can accommodate all.

Sendak, Maurice. *Where the Wild Things Are*. New York: Harper & Row, 1963. *In the Night Kitchen*. New York: Harper & Row, 1970. *Nutshell Library; Alligators All Around; Chicken Soup with Rice; One Was Johnny, Pierre*. New York: Harper & Row, 1962.

Sendak, an award-winning illustrator and writer, has a number of wonderful children's books. Our favorite, *Where the Wild Things Are*, is the story of a little boy sent to his room for misbehaving. He imagines that he sails off to the place where the wild things, a rowdy bunch of monsters, live. He fearlessly confronts them and becomes the king, but then he returns home, where he finds a bowl of hot soup waiting.

Seuss, Dr. *How the Grinch Stole Christmas*. New York: Random House, 1957. *The Sneetches & Other Stories*. New York: Random House, 1961.

These are only two of the many wonderful stories written by Dr. Seuss. Random House also publishes two series of books that carry Dr. Seuss's name (although they are written by various authors). The Bright & Early Books are for children who can't yet read, although they may be able to recognize some words. The second series, Beginner Books, are beginning reading books for children who already have some reading skills. We highly recommend all of these books.

Sheffield, Margaret. *Where Do Babies Come From?* New York: Alfred A. Knopf, 1973.

This book is frank and informative. Its major assets are the illustrations, which are paintings of realistic-looking people. They are not distorted or idealized, and their realism is not frightening. One of the best books of its kind, it is a good introduction to the topics of sex and birth.

Showers, Paul and Kay. *Before You Were a Baby*. New York: Cromwell, 1968.

This is a very clear and direct explanation of conception and pregnancy. It is perhaps a little clinical. It also leaves a lot of unanswered questions, but it can open up good discussions.

Shulevitz, Uri. *Dawn*. New York: Farrar, Straus & Giroux, 1974.

Watercolor illustrations and quiet words tell the moving story of a young child and his grandfather experiencing dawn.

Skorpen, Liesel Moak. *Old Arthur*. New York: Harper & Row, 1972.

Arthur, an old and seemingly useless farm dog, runs away from a man who sees no other alternative than to kill him. After some misadventures, Arthur ends up the pet of a loving little boy.

Steig, William. *Sylvester and the Magic Pebble*. New York: Simon & Schuster, 1969. *Roland the Minstrel Pig*. New York: Harper & Row, 1968.

Steig's illustrations and stories are delightful. In *Sylvester*, a young donkey finds a magic pebble and accidentally turns himself into a rock. His parents grieve (unfortunately, the aproned mother bursts into tears and has to be comforted while the father takes charge of the search). As time passes, his parents manage to go on about their lives, and in the end, Sylvester is brought back to his natural state. In *Roland*, a young artist sets out to follow his creative urges. Despite trials and tribulations, he triumphs. The author also has other excellent titles.

Stein, Sara Bonnett. Open Family Books for Parents and Children Together: *A Hospital Story; About Dying; That New Baby; Making Babies; About Handicaps*. New York: Walker, 1974.

This is an excellent series dealing sensitively with "tender topics." A text for adults offering sound and direct advice appears throughout the book. The book on handicaps is particularly helpful and is one of the few children's books that deal with this topic.

Steptoe, John. *Stevie*. New York: Harper & Row, 1969. *My Special Best Words*. New York: Viking, 1974.

Superlative illustrations and very real stories make these books favorites in our classrooms.

Stevie is a demanding little boy who is cared for each day by Robert's mother. Sibling rivalries arise when Stevie messes up Robert's room and breaks a toy or two. But when Stevie's family moves away, Robert remembers the good times they had and misses his little friend.

My Special Best Words is somewhat controversial in its use of graphic descriptions of bodily functions and black dialect, but we have had great success with it, sparking discussions of language, toilet training, and sibling relationships.

Steven, Carla. *The Birth of Sunset's Kittens*. New York: Young Scott Books, 1969.

A clear and sensitive book that is an excellent lead-in to the topic of birth. Though the book discusses the birth of kittens, the transition to information about humans is well made.

Storm, Hyemeyohsts. *Seven Arrows*. New York: Harper & Row, 1972.

Intended for adult readers, this narrative of Native American life from the entry of the "white man" to the Indians' demise has many allegorical tales that children love. "The Tale of Jumping Mouse" is particularly appealing.

Thomas, Ulrich. *Applemouse*. New York: Hill & Wang, 1972.

This is a charming photographic tale of a mouse building an unlikely house in an apple.

Undry, Janice May. *Mary Jo's Grandmother*. Chicago: Albert Whitman, 1970.

One Christmas, Mary Jo visits her old but independent grandmother, who lives alone in the country. This middle-class black family is loving, warm, and caring.

Van Woerkom, Dorothy. *The Queen Who Couldn't Bake Gingerbread*. New York: Alfred A. Knopf, 1975.

A King who wants a beautiful, wise wife who can bake gingerbread marries a Queen who wants a husband who can play slide trombone. Neither have found the mate they had fantasized, but in the end, the King bakes his own gingerbread and the Queen learns to play the trombone.

Viorst, Judith. *Alexander and the Terrible, Horrible, No Good, Very Bad Day*. New York: Atheneum, 1976. *I'll Fix Anthony*. New York: Harper & Row, 1969. *Rosie and Michael*. New York: Atheneum, 1974. *The Tenth Good Thing about Barney*. New York: Atheneum, 1971.

The first three books may not give earth-shattering and meaningful solutions and insights into problems of sibling rivalry and friendship between the sexes, but they add an important element to tricky situations—humor.

The Tenth Good Thing About Barney deals sensitively with death, loss, and separation. It is the story of a boy coping with the death of his pet cat, Barney.

Waber, Bernard. *Ira Sleeps Over*. New York: Houghton Mifflin, 1972.

Indecisive about bringing his teddy bear on his first overnight visit to a friend's house, Ira, in response to his sister's taunts, leaves his bear at home. Ira is surprised and relieved when his friend sneaks his own teddy bear out of a drawer. Ira returns home (next door) to retrieve his own. In addition to allowing little boys to have and deal with emotional needs, this book presents the rest of the family in nonstereotyped ways. The author is best known for his books about Lyle the Crocodile. His earlier books are full of sex stereotypes in an all-white world. The later ones have integrated casts of characters and more liberated roles for women and girls. Comparing the earlier and later stories can be fascinating.

Waxman, Stephanie. *What Is a Boy? What Is a Girl?* Los Angeles: Peace Press, 1977.

A frank and forthright book illustrated with photos of nude humans, both adult and children, that deals with physical differences between the sexes. Non-sexist and sensitive, it deals with typical children's questions: "Will I grow one?" "Will mine fall off?" "Will I always be a boy/girl?" Although marred by the curious fact that the author uses the wrong terminology for female genitalia, it is otherwise an excellent, only-one-of-its-kind book.

Wirsen, C. *A Child Is Born—A Drama of Life before Birth*. New York: Dell, 1969.

This book is illustrated with incredibly beautiful color photos of the developing fetus.

Young, Jim. *When the Whale Came to My Town*. New York: Alfred A. Knopf, 1974.

A little boy discovers a beached and ailing whale. Even though the Coast Guard and doctors work tirelessly for three days in an attempt to save the animal, it dies, but not before the little boy offers hope and solace to the massive creature. In so doing, the boy learns that there can be beauty in death and saying good-bye.

Zolotow, Charlotte. *A Father Like That*. Illustrated by Ben Shecter. New York: Harper & Row, 1971. *William's Doll*. New York: Harper & Row, 1972. *My Grandson Lew*. New York: Harper & Row, 1972.

Zolotow has written several wonderful books which we use in our homes and classrooms. These are three of our favorites.

In *A Father Like That*, a little boy idealizes a fantasy of his missing father. With honesty and warmth, the mother tells her son that just in case he never gets a father like that, he can be that kind of father when he grows up.

William's Doll is the story of a boy who wants a doll, to his father's dismay. When William's grandmother comes to visit, she buys him a doll so he can learn to be a nurturing, caring father when he grows up.

My Grandson Lew is one of Zolotow's best. Lew misses his grandfather, who has died. Through sharing good memories, Lew and his mother feel closer to the grandfather and cope positively with their feelings of loss.

Bibliographies of Children's Literature

Bernstein, Joanne E. *Books to Help Children Cope with Separation and Loss*. New York: R. R. Bowker, 1977.

Davis, Enid. *The Liberty Cap*. Chicago: Academy Press, 1977.

Rudman, Masha K. *Children's Literature*. Lexington, Mass: D. C. Heath, 1976.

Bibliography of Open Education

Blackie, John. *Inside the Primary School*. London: Her Majesty's Stationery Office, 1967.

Holt, John. *What Do I Do on Monday?* New York: Dell, 1970.

Silberman, Charles. *The Open Classroom Reader*. New York: Random House, 1973.

Word Family List

ab: cab, dab, gab, jab, lab, nab, tab, grab
ad: bad, cad, dad, fad, lad, mad, pad, sad, glad
ag: bag, gag, lag, nag, rag, sag, tag, brag, wag, crag, drag, flag, snag
am: am, dam, ham, jam, Pam, ram, Sam, clam, sham, slam, tram, scram
an: an, ban, can, Dan, fan, man, Nan, pan, ran, tan, van, bran, plan
ap: cap, gap, lap, map, nap, rap, sap, tap, chap, clap, slap, snap, trap
ar: bar, car, far, jar, tar
at: at, bat, cat, fat, hat, mat, pat, rat, sat, vat, drat, flat, slat, that
ay: bay, day, hay, jay, lay, May, pay, ray, say, way, clay, gray, play
ed: bed, fed, led, red, Ted, wed, bled, fled, shed, sled
eg: beg, keg, leg, peg
en: Ben, den, hen, men, pen, ten, glen, then, when
et: bet, get, jet, let, met, net, pet, set, vet, wet
id: bid, did, hid, kid, lid, rid, skid, slid
ig: big, dig, fig, jig, pig, rig, wig
in: in, bin, din, fin, kin, pin, sin, tin, win, chin, grin, shin, skin, spin, thin, twin
ip: dip, hip, lip, rip, sip, tip
it: it, bit, fit, hit, kit, lit, pit, sit, wit, flit, knit, quit, slit, spit
ob: Bob, cob, job, lob, mob, rob, sob, blob, slob, snob
op: bop, cop, hop, mop, pop, top
ot: cot, dot, got, hot, jot, lot, not, pot, rot, tot, blot, clot, knot, plot, shot, slot, spot, trot
ub: cub, hub, rub, sub, tub
ud: bud, cud, dud, mud, spud, thud
ug: bug, dug, hug, jug, rug, tug
um: bum, gum, hum, rum, sum
un: bun, fun, gun, nun, run, sun, shun, spun, stun
up: up, cup, pup, sup
ut: but, cut, gut, hut, jut, nut, rut

ack: back, hack, jack, lack, pack, sack, black, quack, stack, smack, snack, track, shack
age: cage, page, sage, rage, wage, stage
aid: braid, maid, paid, raid
ake: bake, cake, fake, lake, make, rake, sake, take, wake, stake, brake, flake, snake, quake, shake
and: and, band, hand, land, bland, brand, grand, stand
eat: eat, beat, feat, heat, meat, neat, peat, seat, bleat, cheat, pleat, treat, wheat
eed: deed, feed, need, seed, weed, bleed, greed, speed
eek: meek, peek, seek, creek, cheek, sleek
eel: feel, heel, peel, steel, wheel

eep: beep, deep, jeep, keep, peep, seep, weep, creep, sleep, sweep, sheep
eet: beet, feet, meet, greet, sheet, tweet
ent: bent, dent, lent, rent, sent, tent, vent, went, spent
ile: file, mile, pile, tile, while
ine: dine, fine, line, mine, nine, pine, vine, wine, shine, spine, twine, whine
ing: ding, king, ring, sing, wing, bring, cling, fling, sting, swing
ink: link, mink, pink, sink, wink, blink, brink, clink, drink, stink, think
int: hint, lint, mint, tint, flint, stint
oil: oil, boil, coil, foil, soil, broil, spoil
oke: Coke, joke, poke, woke, broke, choke, smoke, spoke
old: old, bold, cold, fold, gold, hold, mold, sold, told, scold
ook: book, cook, hook, look, nook, took, brook, crook, shook
ool: cool, pool, tool, spool, stool
ore: ore, bore, core, more, sore, tore, chore, shore, store
orn: born, corn, horn, morn, worn, sworn
unk: bunk, dunk, hunk, junk, sunk, chunk, clunk, drunk, skunk, spunk, stunk, trunk

Silent E List

bit/bite
can/cane
cap/cape
cod/code
con/cone
cub/cube
cut/cute
dim/dime
fad/fade
fin/fine
fir/fire
gal/gale
glob/globe
grad/grade
Jan/Jane
hat/hate
hid/hide
hop/hope
kit/kite
mad/made
man/mane
not/note
pal/pale
pin/pine
plan/plane
pop/pope
quit/quite
rid/ride
rip/ripe
rob/robe
Sam/same
sham/shame
scrap/scrape
slat/slate
slid/slide
slop/slope
spit/spite
strip/stripe
tap/tape
Tim/time
ton/tone
tub/tube
twin/twine
van/vane
wad/wade
win/wine

Consonant Blends and Digraphs

Blends

bl: blue, blade, bless, bluff, blank, blink, black, bleat, blond, bled, bleed, blood, blend, blare, blunt, blurt, block, blind, blame, blaze, bleak, blade, blow, blew, bland *cl*: clock, claim, club, clan, clean, clip, clap, clot, clear, clash, clay, clam, Clark, clerk, click, claw, clod, clump, clove, close, climb, cliff, clan, class, cling, clip

fl: float, flop, flee, flow, flame, flag, flit, flea, flute, fled, flour, flog, flick, flight, flare, fly, flask, flirt, fling, flint, flesh, flash, flap, flavor, floor, flake, flip

gl: glue, glass, glee, gleam, glow, gloom, glide, glen, glib, glum, glint, glimmer, glove, glaze, glare, glad, glade, globe, glance, gland

pl: play, plough, plan, plight, plea, plume, plank, plain, plait, plate, plot, please, plum, pluck, pleat, ply, plod, place, plane, plenty, plug

sl: slide, slim, slave, slid, slop, slope, slap, sleep, slip, slick, slay, sleet, sleigh, sled, slam, sleeve, sloop, slight, slinky, sloppy, slur, sling, sleek, slender, slow, slot

br: bred, bread, braid, broke, brink, brand, brake, break, bring, brought, brother, bride, brood, brush, brand, breach, brunch, brick, brown, broil, brim, bridge, brew, bright, breeze, brave, brief

cr: cram, crack, cream, cradle, crib, cry, crane, crawl, creep, crept, crack, cross, crush, crop, crab, crisp, cringe, crust, cramp, crag, crash, craft, crazy, crease, creak, crime, crimp, crate, crow

dr: drank, drab, drag, drake, drape, draw, drown, dress, dream, drew, drink, drill, drip, drift, drive, drop, droop, drool, drove, drunk, drudge, dry

fr: fresh, friend, frank, from, fray, free, frame, frill, fright, fringe, frog, fry, frock, frond, froze, frisky, fret, freak, freeze, frail, France, froth, frown, fruit, fright

gr: grab, grade, grape, grand, grass, gray, graze, great, greed, green, greet, grew, grief, grill, grim, grime, grin, gripe, grit, groan, ground, group, grow, growl, gruff

pr: print, proof, prove, pride, prune, preach, print, prick, prism, prop, prize, price, press, prod, prim, pram, pretty, proud, pray, praise, pry, prime

tr: track, tram, trail, trade, train, tramp, trap, trash, tray, trace, tree, treat, trend, trick, trip, trill, tripe, trim, troupe, troop, true, truck, trunk, try

sc: scare, scant, scat, scan, scab, scar, scarf, scalp, scamper, scold, scowl, score, scoop, scour, scout, scoot, scum

sk: skate, sketch, skew, skin, skinny, skill, skip, skim, skit, skid, ski, skirt, skull, skunk, sky

sm: small, smart, smack, smash, smell, smear, smile, smite, smog, smoke, smooth, smock, smother, smug, smudge, smut

sn: snake, snatch, snap, snack, snag, snail, snarl, sneer, sneak, sneeze, snitch, snip, snide, sniff, snow, snoop, snore, snort, snug, snub

sp: span, spat, spark, spank, spade, spawn, spare, spell, speak, speck, speech, spent, spit, spite, spill, spin, spine, spike, spool, spooky, spot, spoil, sport, spoon, spoke

st: stand, stamp, stay, stain, stall, stake, stag, stab, stage, stalk, stack, start, stare, star, steam, stem, steak, steep, still, sting, stint, store, stood, stop, stone

sw: sway, swat, swank, swell, sweep, sweet, swear, sweat, swim, switch, swift, swipe, swing, swore, swoon, sworn, swoop, swung

Digraphs

ch: chair, chase, cheep, cheek, check, cheap, chin, chick, chose, choose, choke, choice, church, chug, chase, chime, charm, chip, chat, chop, chest, chap, champ, chum, chill, chimp, chunk
gh: laugh, enough, though, through, rough, tough
ng: bang, bring, cling, ding, fling, flung, king, ping, rung, ring, song, sing, sung, sang, swing, spring, sprang, sting, sling, string, thing, wring, wrung, lung, fang, gang, hang, rang, slang, clang, wing, hung
ph: phone, phase, photo
qu: quit, quite, quiet, quick, queen, question, quarrel, quill, queer, quake, quack
sh: shall, shake, sham, shame, shell, sheep, shepherd, shine, show, ship, shoe, shelf, shod, shop, shin, shave, shed, shut, shun, shot, shape, shone, shore, shark, short, shirt, shag
th: thin, the, there, they, their, those, that, this, then, than, these, thousand, thank, thunder, throw, through, threw, though, thing, thimble, thick, thump, throat, thorn
tw: twain, twang, twelve, tweet, tweed, twenty, tweak, twin, twig, twill, twice, twirl, twist, twine, twitch, twinkle
wh: what, whale, whack, wheat, wheel, where, when, whim, whip, while, white, whine, which, whiff, why

Beyond Introductory Phonics

Consonant Irregularities

Luckily, the sounds represented by consonants are much more regular than those made by vowels. There are, however, some variations. The only ones that are likely to become a problem in beginning reading are the hard and soft sounds of the letters *g* and *c* and the digraphs. Even though we don't teach any of the other variations as rules, it helps if you are familiar with these rules so that you can deal with questions as they arise.

1. The letter *c* is sounded as a *k* when followed by the vowels *a, o,* or *u* and as an *s* when followed by *i, e,* or *y*.

2. The letter *g* has a hard sound when followed by *a, e,* or *o*. It often has a soft sound, like the letter *j*, when followed by *i, e,* or *y*.

3. The letter *s* most often makes the sound heard in the words *sing, set, soap,* and *sun*. Sometimes *s* is sounded as a *z* in one-syllable words: *is, his, cheese, please*. It can also be sounded as *sh* as in *sure* or *sugar*.

4. The letter *x* usually has the sounds of *ks (box, tax, six)*, but never when it begins a word.

5. When *y* begins a word, it acts as a consonant *(yes, yard, yellow)*. In one-syllable words, it can act as a vowel and is sounded like a long *i (by, cry, sly)*.

6. When two consonants appear together, one of them may be silent. When *b* follows *m*, the *b* is usually silent *(lamb, comb)*. When *t* follows *b*, the *b* is usually silent *(doubt, debt)*. When a vowel follows *gh*, the *h* is usually silent *(ghost)*. If a vowel precedes *gh*, the *gh* is silent *(light, taught, weight)*. When *d, m,* or *k* follow *l*, the *l* is usually silent *(would, talk, palm)*. When *s* follows *p*, the *p* is usually silent *(psalm, psychic)*. When *r* follows *w*, the *w* is usually silent *(wrong)*. When *ch* follows *t*, the *t* is usually silent *(witch, watch)*. In words beginning with *kn*, the *k* is usually silent *(know, knock)*. In words ending with the syllable *ten*, the *t* is often not sounded.

Vowel Irregularities

There is a considerable amount of variation in the sounds vowels and vowel combinations can make. There are some generalized rules, but alas, they are full of variations and exceptions. Still, if you are aware of the general rules, and the general categories of variations, you can at least have something impressive to say when a child wants to know why a particular vowel sound is neither long nor short when you told him each vowel had two sounds.

1. A single vowel in a medial position in a word or syllable usually has a short sound, except for the following instances:

a. The vowel *a* sounds like *aw* when it is followed by *l, ll, w,* or *u* *(wolf, draw, tall)*.

b. The vowel *i* followed by *nd, ld,* or *gh* often has its long sound *(find, light, child)*.

c. The vowel *o* followed by *ld* usually has its long sound *(sold, old, cold)*.

d. A vowel followed by *r* makes a sound that is neither long nor short *(car, her, for)*.

e. The letters *ir* are usually pronounced *ur (bird)* except when followed by a final *e (fire)*.

2. When two vowels come together, the first one generally has its long sound and the second one is silent. This rule has a number of exceptions, but holds up well for *ee, oa, ea,* and *ai*.

3. In words with two vowels, one of which is a final *e*, the *e* is usually silent and the other vowel has its long sound *(fine, hate, cape)*.

4. The letters *ay* at the end of a word generally has the long sound of *a*.

5. When the only vowel in a word or accented syllable comes at the end of that word or syllable, it usually has a long sound.

6. The combination *ow* is sometimes pronounced as a long *o (tow)*.

7. Vowel diphthongs are two vowels that come together and make a separate vowel sound. Diphthongs do not follow the general rule for two vowels (rule 2) but make a speech sound of their own *(boy, boil, plow)*.

Basic Vocabulary List

Remedial-Reading Vocabulary for Primary Grades

The following list of 754 words was compiled for use in preparing for older children suitable remedial-reading materials with a vocabulary at the primary-grade level. It was derived by first selecting the words of highest frequency in the Faucett-Maki list. These were then checked against the International Kindergarten Union list and the Fitzgerald list in order to make sure that the words finally included are known and used by children.

The list contains 90 percent of the words ordinarily used in the written compositions of children in the intermediate grades and is therefore also useful as a remedial-spelling list.

Complete Alphabetical List of 754 Words

The number before each word indicates its frequency; for example, 1 means that the word is among the most frequently used words in the list, while 7 means that it is least frequently used at this level.

1 a
7 able
1 about
3 above
7 absent
6 across
7 act
7 add
6 address
4 afraid
3 after
6 afternoon
2 again
3 against
4 ago
7 ahead
6 air
7 alike
7 alive
1 all
4 almost
3 alone
3 along
5 already

5 also
7 although
4 always
3 am
7 among
7 amount
2 an
1 and
7 angry
4 animal
3 another
3 answer
2 any
7 anybody
5 anything
7 apart
7 apple
1 are
5 arm
4 around
2 as
3 ask
7 asleep
1 at

4 ate
2 away
7 awful

4 baby
2 back
4 bad
5 bag
4 ball
7 bank
5 barn
4 basket
2 be
3 bear
7 beat
5 beautiful
4 because
3 bed
3 been
3 before
6 beg
4 began
6 begin
5 behind

4 being
4 believe
5 bell
7 belong
3 best
2 better
3 between
1 big
7 bill
3 bird
4 birthday
5 bit
3 black
5 blow
3 blue
5 board
4 boat
6 body
3 book
7 born
3 both
7 bother
7 bottom
7 bought

5 box
2 boy
5 bread
6 break
7 bridge
5 bright
4 bring
7 broken
5 brother
6 brought
3 brown
7 brush
6 build
7 burn
7 business
5 busy
2 but
7 button
4 buy
2 by

2 call
2 came
1 can
7 candy
6 can't
5 cap
3 car
6 card
4 care
4 carry
6 case
3 cat
3 catch
7 caught
6 cause
7 cent
7 certain
3 chair
4 change
5 child
3 children
7 choose
7 church
4 city
6 class
4 clean
6 clear
7 climb
3 close
7 cloth
7 clothes
5 coat
4 cold
7 college
6 color
2 come
5 company
7 cook
7 cool
6 copy
5 cost
2 could
7 count
4 country
5 course
3 cover
6 cross
5 cry
7 cup
3 cut

5 dance
5 dark
2 day
6 dead
7 decide
6 deep
2 did
6 didn't
6 die
5 different
6 dig
4 dinner
1 do
7 doctor
3 does
7 doesn't
3 dog
7 dollar
4 done
5 don't
3 door
2 down
5 draw
5 dress
5 drink
6 drive
6 drop
7 dry
7 during

4 each
5 ear
4 early
6 east
3 eat
4 egg
6 eight
4 either
6 else
4 end
4 enough
3 even
4 evening
5 ever
4 every
5 everything
6 except
7 excuse
5 expect
3 eye

5 face
4 fair
4 fall
6 family
3 far
4 farm
3 fast
7 fat
4 father
7 fed
5 feed
3 feel
5 feet
5 fell
6 felt
4 few
5 field
7 fight
5 fill
3 find
3 fine
7 finger
6 finish
4 fire
3 first
6 fit
5 five
6 fix
5 floor
5 flower
5 fly
7 fold
7 follow
7 food
6 foot
1 for
6 forget
7 forgot
3 found
3 four
7 free
3 friend
2 from
6 front
7 fruit
5 full
5 fun
7 funny

5 game
5 garden
3 gave
2 get
3 girl
2 give
4 glad
7 glass
1 go
7 gold
5 gone
2 good
3 got
7 grade
3 gray
4 great
4 green
7 grew
5 ground
5 grow
3 guess

2 had
3 hair
3 half
3 hand
7 handle
7 hang
7 happen
4 happy
3 hard
7 hardly
3 has
6 hat
1 have
7 haven't
1 he
3 head
3 hear
3 heard
6 heart
6 heavy
5 held

2 help
2 her
2 here
5 hide
4 high
5 hill
2 him
1 his
5 hit
4 hold
5 hole
4 home
3 hope
7 horn
5 horse
5 hot
7 hour
2 house
2 how
4 hundred
5 hungry
7 hunt
7 hurry
7 hurt

1 I
7 idea
3 if
5 I'll
1 in
7 inside
6 instead
7 interest
2 into
7 iron
1 is
1 it
2 its

5 jump
2 just

3 keep
4 kept
7 kick
7 kill
5 kind
5 knew
7 knock
3 know

6 lady
4 land
5 large
3 last
4 late
3 laugh
4 lay
6 lead
4 learn
7 least
5 leave
5 left
6 leg
2 let
3 letter
7 lie
7 life
7 lift
4 light
2 like
4 line
7 listen
1 little
3 live
2 long
2 look
7 lose
5 lost
5 lot
3 love
6 low

2 made
6 mail
2 make
2 man
2 many
6 mark
3 matter
2 may
1 me
2 mean
7 measure
7 meat
3 meet
5 men
7 middle
3 might
6 mile
3 milk
4 mind
6 mine
5 minute
4 miss
7 mistake
7 mix
5 money
4 month
3 more
3 morning
3 most
3 mother
7 mountain
5 move
3 Mr.
5 Mrs.
3 much
6 music
2 must
1 my
6 myself

3 name
3 near
4 need
3 never
3 new
7 news

6 next
6 nice
3 night
7 nine
2 no
7 nobody
5 noise
7 nor
7 north
7 nose
1 not
6 note
3 nothing
2 now
5 number

7 o'clock
1 of
3 off
7 office
5 often
3 oh
2 old
1 on
3 once
1 one
4 only
3 open
3 or
7 order
3 other
6 ought
4 our
1 out
2 over
4 own

6 page
7 paid
7 paint
4 paper
4 part
5 party
4 pass
6 past
3 pay
7 pencil
4 people
7 person
7 pick
5 picture
5 piece
4 place
7 plan
6 plant
2 play
2 please
4 point
5 poor
7 possible
7 pound
7 pour
7 practice
3 present
4 pretty
7 price
6 print
4 pull
7 push
2 put

6 quick
5 quiet
6 quite

3 rabbit
5 rain
2 ran
6 rather
4 reach
4 read
5 ready
6 real
7 really
4 reason
7 receive
3 red
4 remember
4 rest
7 rich
5 ride
4 right
5 ring
6 river
5 road
7 rock
4 roll
4 room
4 round
7 rubber
7 rule
2 run

7 sad
7 safe
2 said
7 sail
7 sale
3 same
4 sat
6 save
2 saw
2 say
3 school
6 sea
7 seat
4 second
1 see
3 seem
5 seen
5 sell
3 send
4 sent
4 set
6 seven
4 several
7 sew
5 shake
5 shall
1 she
7 shine
6 ship
5 shoe
7 shoot
4 short
7 shot
5 should
4 show
7 shut
6 sick
5 side
6 sign
6 silk
7 since
4 sing
7 sir
5 sister
5 sit
4 six
7 size
7 skin
3 sleep
7 slip
7 slow
5 small
7 smoke
5 snow
2 so
7 soft
6 sold
2 some
4 something
5 sometime
7 son
5 song
3 soon
7 sorry
6 sound
6 south
5 speak
7 spend
7 spoil

6 spring
7 stamp
4 stand
7 star
4 start
7 state
7 station
5 stay
7 steal
6 step
3 still
7 stitch
5 stone
3 stop
6 store
3 story
7 straight
7 strange
4 street
5 strong
7 struck
7 study
3 such
6 suit
4 summer
5 sun
7 supper
5 suppose
3 sure
5 surprise
6 sweet
7 swim

4 table
2 take
4 talk
6 teach
7 teeth
2 tell
4 ten
4 than
2 thank
1 that
1 the
3 their
1 them
2 then
1 there
5 these
1 they
3 thing
3 think
5 third
2 this
4 those
6 though
5 thought
6 thousand
3 three
7 threw
7 through
7 throw
7 tie
4 till
2 time
7 tire
1 to
4 today
4 together
5 told
5 tomorrow
2 too
3 took
5 top
6 touch
4 town
7 trade
4 train
3 tree
7 trip
7 trouble
4 true
3 try
4 turn
2 two

3 under
7 understand
3 until
1 up
4 upon
2 us
3 use

3 very
6 visit

7 wagon
4 wait
3 walk
6 wall
2 want
6 war
5 warm
1 was
6 wash
5 watch
2 water
3 way
1 we
6 wear
6 weather
4 week
7 weigh
2 well
1 went
2 were
6 west
7 wet
1 what
2 when
2 where
6 whether
1 which
5 while
3 white
2 who
4 whole
7 whom
6 whose
2 why
6 wide
1 will
5 win
5 wind
5 window
5 winter
3 wish
1 with
3 without
5 woman
6 wonder
7 won't
5 wood
4 word
3 work
6 world
2 would
7 wouldn't
7 wrap
3 write
7 written
6 wrong
6 wrote

5 yard
3 year
4 yellow
3 yes
6 yesterday
4 yet
1 you
3 young
2 your
6 yourself

Alphabet Patterns

ABCD

EFGHI

JKLM

NOPQR

STUV

WXYZ

INDEX

WITHDRAWN
LAKEWOOD MEMORIAL LIBRARY
LAKEWOOD, NEW YORK 14750